Christmas Traditions Quilt

Quilt Block Party Series Number Four

by

Wendy Gilbert

a Quilt in a Day® Publication

Introduction

Christmas is a holiday surrounded by a wealth of traditions and customs. As a quilter, I dreamed about a sampler Christmas quilt my family could display during the month of December. My wish was to design a quilt that would include many of the traditions shared by families everywhere.

Then in 1991, Eleanor Burns asked me to teach Quilt in a Day's Block of the Month. I seized the opportunity and challenged 75 Block of the Month quiltmakers to join in the event. We met each month and by December we had designed, sewn, and finished our beautiful heirloom Christmas quilts.

The universal reaction to the quilt was that it was a challenging but rewarding experience. Every quiltmaker declared her sewing skills improved tremendously. Of course, not everyone made a big quilt. Some students made smaller projects from their favorite blocks. It's a great quilt to let your imagination go--the possibilities are endless.

Now it's your turn to sew an heirloom for your family to enjoy. Let your Christmas Traditions Quilt reflect the true meaning of Christmas for years to come.

Merry Christmas!

Wendy Gilbert, 1992

Table of Contents

Fabric Selection

Consider:
A scrap "look" or a planned "look" to the quilt?
An old fashioned look or a contemporary look?
Whether the Picture Blocks or the Chain
Blocks will stand out or be equal in value?
Traditional Christmas colors or colors to
blend with home decor?

Choose your Chain Fabric First

A solid color or a fabric that appears solid from a distance will result in a more dominant chain.

A small scale multicolor fabric results in a more subtle chain.

A multicolor fabric with light results in a light airy feeling.

A large scale print works well but adds a busier look.

Avoid directional fabrics.

Decide if binding will be the same as the chain or a contrasting fabric.

Choose your Background Fabric Second

Fabric that is plain or has a very simple design so it won't compete with the Picture Blocks.

Fabric that is non-directional to avoid cutting problems. Check closely, direction can be deceiving. Also, yardage is not allowed for directional fabric.

Closely woven fabric. Loosely woven fabrics are much more difficult to work with.

Choose your Picture Fabrics Last

A minimum of four red and four green fabrics are needed.

Purchase new fabric or use fabrics from your collection.

In the quilt, any red or green fabric will look like a Christmas fabric.

Three blocks have bows on them that require two shades of one color. Contrast is important. Sometimes the reverse side of a fabric will work.

Select fabrics that vary in pattern size and design.

Directional fabrics should be avoided except as an accent in a few blocks. They will require extra planning, cutting skill, and extra yardage.

Think about the color of your reds and greens. Do you want to stay within the same color family, such as red fabric with blue or orange tones, and green fabric with blue or yellow tones?

All main fabrics, purchased or from your collection, should be 45" wide. Accent fabrics can be scraps.

Yardage

Select good quality 100% cotton fabrics 45" wide.

Chain Fabric	1¼ yards
Background Fabric Picture Blocks & Chain Blocks	7 yards total 3½ yards each
Picture Block Main Fabrics	2 yards total or 8 to 10 - ¼ yard pieces
Picture Block Accent Fabrics Recommended: Gold, Brown, Tan	Scraps or ⅛ yard each
Binding Fabric Same as Chain or Contrasting	1½ yards
Backing Fabric 45" wide 108" wide	 5 yards or 2⅓ yards
Bonded Lightweight Batting	84" x 84"
Flannel Board Materials ⅔ yard light colored flannel 18" x 22" cardboard Tape 22" x 26" lightweight batting scrap	Wrap cardboard first with batting and then with flannel. Tape on reverse side. Place each picture block piece as it is cut, on the flannel board in rows.

Other Supplies:

- Marking pencils for light and dark fabrics
- 6" x 6" ruler
- 6" x 12" ruler
- 6" x 24" ruler
- 12½" Square Up ruler
- Industrial size rotary cutter
- Gridded cutting mat
- Thread
- Fine nylon invisible thread (optional)
- Extra long quilter's pins
- Walking foot attachment
- 1" safety pins
- ¼" masking tape, or sharp dry piece of soap
- Bicycle clips (optional)
- Template plastic (optional)

General Cutting & Sewing Suggestions

Before cutting, study the color drawing of each block. Then choose the fabrics for your block. Remember color placement is only a suggestion.

Cut the fabrics in the order listed in the Fabric Cutting Instruction charts.

For most fabrics, first cut a 45" strip and then cut the strip into pieces.

If the fabric does not call for a 45" strip, cut the individual pieces.

In some cases you will need to cut both a 45" strip and individual pieces from one fabric.

Pieces are listed "width by the length" in the Cutting Instruction charts.

Cut 45" selvage to selvage strips from one side of the fabric and individual pieces from the opposite side.

In the Fabric Cutting Instruction charts, each piece is assigned a "letter" as well as a "row number" which correspond with the Layout Diagram of that block.

The best approach is to cut each piece and immediately place it on your flannel board according to its "letter and row number" as shown on the Layout Diagram. Number the rows with masking tape.

Save any scraps for future blocks.

If strips are not 45" you may need extra.

From the Background Fabric, cut off 3 ½ yards for the chain background and set aside.

From the remaining 3 ½ yards of Background Fabric for the picture blocks, cut off one yard pieces for an easier amount to handle.

Trim selvages before cutting pieces from 45" strips.

As you cut, check off each piece on the cutting page.

Each picture block is cut and then sewn.

Important

Most sewing problems are the result of incorrectly cut pieces.

✂ Cutting Instructions

Cut from the background fabric:

(1) 2 ½" x 45"--cut into:
    (2) 2 ½" x 13 ½" 1a,8a
    (2) 2 ½" x 3 ¼" 2f
    (2) 2" x 2 ½" 6o
(1) 1 ½" x 45"--cut into:
    (2) 1 ½" x 4" 2b
    (2) 1 ¼" x 4 ¾" 3i
    (2) 1 ¼" x 6 ¾" 7q
    (1) 1 ½" x 3 ½" 2d
(2) 2" x 4" 5m
(2) 3" x 4" 4k

$1^{1/2}$" x 4" $1^{1/4}$"x 4$^{3/4}$", $1^{1/4}$"x 6$^{3/4}$"   ,$1^{1/2}$"x3$^{1/2}$"

folded strip

2 $^{1/2}$" x 45"

1 $^{1/2}$" x 45"

(2) 2 "x 4"   (2) 3"x 4"

6

The Scant ¼" Seam Test

Do Not Skip This Step!

This is the most important step before starting to sew this quilt!

Sewing Suggestions

- Use a fine sharp, #10 (American) or #70 (European), needle.
- Use a neutral color thread, white, beige, or gray. Dark thread for sewing parts of the blocks may be preferred so that light stitching does not show.
- Use small stitches, approximately 15 per inch.
- Use the same sewing machine throughout this quilt.
- Do not backstitch, except where indicated.
- Complete the **Scant ¼" Seam Test** before starting.

The picture blocks were first drafted on graph paper. A ¼" seam allowance was then added to each piece. However, if the blocks are sewn with an exact ¼" seam they will not fit together properly because no allowance was made for the fold in the fabrics that occurs when two pieces are stitched and pressed. Therefore, the solution to this problem is to complete the Scant ¼" Seam Test so your seams will be a scant smaller than ¼" and allow for the fabric fold.

Do not guess at a scant ¼" seam. If you skip this test you will have problems throughout the sewing of this quilt.

1. Using the rotary cutter and ruler, accurately cut a 1½" x 45" strip of background fabric.

2. Cut off (3) 1½" x 6" pieces from the 45" strip.

3. Sew the three strips together lengthwise with what you think is a scant ¼" seam.

4. Press the seams in one direction. Make sure no folds occur at the seam when pressing.

5. Place the sewn sample under a ruler and measure its width. It should measure exactly 3½" wide. If sample measures smaller than 3½", seam is too large. If sample measures larger than 3½", seam is too small.

6. Adjust seam allowance and repeat if necessary. Do not cheat!

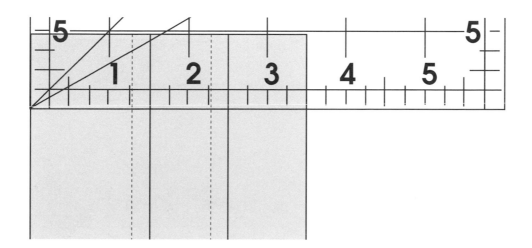

General Techniques Used Throughout the Book

Diagonal Sewing Technique

This method is used to sew a 45° angle between two fabrics.

Follow specific directions and diagrams for individual blocks.

1. Flip pieces, right sides together, according to block diagrams.

2. Using a sharp pencil and a 6" x 6" ruler, draw a diagonal line on the wrong side of fabric as shown.

   Hint: Move the background piece in slightly while marking the diagonal. This makes the marking easier and more accurate. Then reposition the piece before sewing.

3. Press the two fabrics together to hold them in place.

4. Place your needle, at the edge of the fabric, lined up with one of the pencil lines. Hold your threads and sew in the direction of the arrow.

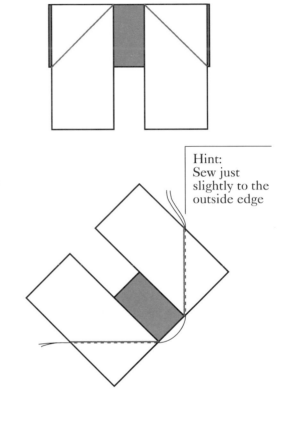

Hint: Sew just slightly to the outside edge

5. Open out the fabric and check to make sure the two sewn pieces have come out even. If edges are uneven, carefully unsew and try again.

Correct

Incorrect

6. Trim seams to ¼".

7. Press seams according to block directions.

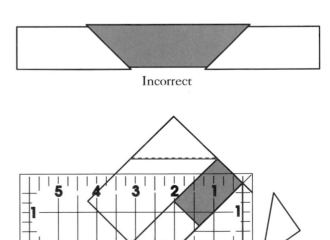

Stabilizing Pin Technique

This technique is used to match a diagonal seam to a straight seam.

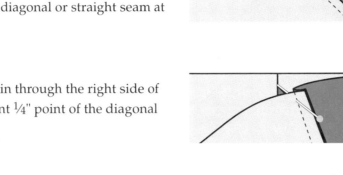

1. Working from the wrong side of the first fabric, push a stabilizing pin through the diagonal or straight seam at the scant ¼" point.

2. Next, push the stabilizing pin through the right side of the second fabric at the scant ¼" point of the diagonal or straight seam.

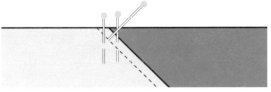

3. Leaving the stabilizing pin standing "straight up" in the fabric, pin on both sides of it. Remove stabilizing pin.

4. Sew.

5. Check right side for accuracy.

Press As You Sew

After sewing each seam, press according to the directions. Seams are pressed in the direction they lie best or pressed so they will lock together with a seam from another row.

Setting the Seams

Seams should always be pressed flat or "set" first and then pressed in the direction the instructions indicate.

Assembly-Line Sewing

Assembly-line sewing is a method of sewing that saves time and thread. To start, with right sides together, pick up your first pair of pieces. After sewing them together, do not lift the presser foot or clip the threads. Butt and stitch the second pair immediately behind the first. Butt and stitch all remaining pairs together in the same manner. Cut pairs apart.

Sliver Trimming

Sliver trimming refers to the trimming that may be necessary when edges are slightly uneven after sewing. Sliver trimming may be necessary at any time throughout the construction of the quilt. Sliver trimming may be needed for sewn pieces or whole rows to make fitting the blocks together easier. Remember it is called sliver trimming because you remove only a sliver of fabric.

Locking the Seams

Seams are pressed in opposite directions so they will lock together when the rows of the block are sewn.

The Tree

Cut from tree fabric:

(1) 4" x 45"--cut into:
- (1) 4" x 9 ½" 4g
- (1) 3" x 7 ½" 3e
- (1) 3" x 5 ½" 2c

Cut from trunk fabric:

(1) 2" x 2 ½" 5i

Cut from the background fabric:

(1) 2 ½" x 45"--cut into:
- (2) 2 ½" x 13 ½" 1a,6a
- (2) 2" x 6" 5h

(1) 4" x 45"--cut into:
- (2) 4" x 6" 4f
- (2) 3" x 7" 2b
- (2) 3" x 6" 3d

Throughout time, the evergreen tree has come to represent renewed life. While other trees stand bare and gray in December, the evergreen flourishes with winter fruits of cones and berries. For this reason, the German people selected the evergreen tree as a symbol of Christ. Their custom of decorating small tabletop Christmas trees came to America when the German people immigrated about the time of the Revolutionary War. Large floor to ceiling trees then became popular in timber-rich America. Few things are as inviting and friendly as the Christmas tree. It links Christmas past and present, while holding a very personal meaning for each family.

❏ Layout Diagram

Lay the cut pieces as shown in this diagram:

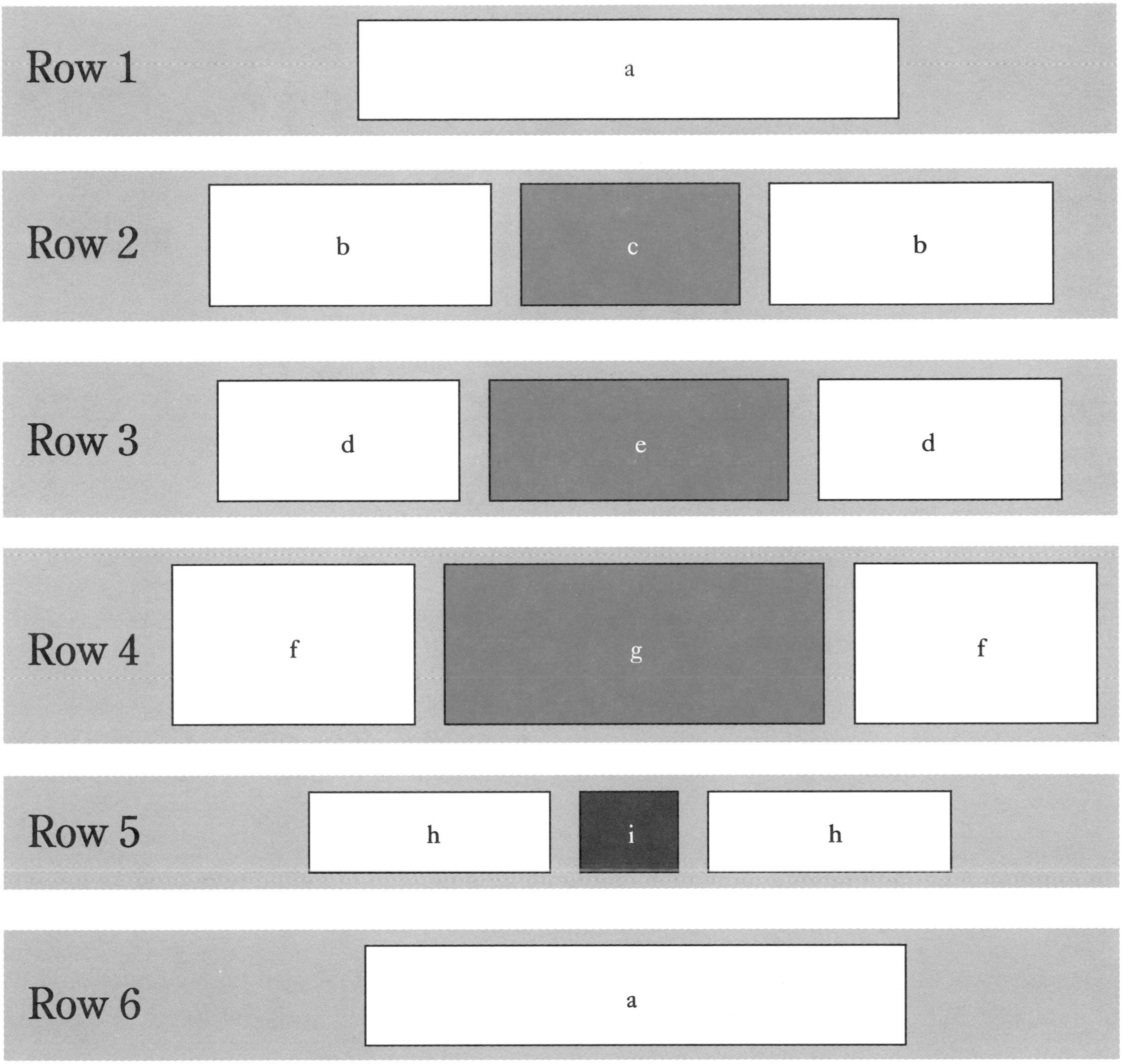

Row 1

a

Row 2

b   c   b

Row 3

d   e   d

Row 4

f   g   f

Row 5

h   i   h

Row 6

a

Sewing the Tree Block

Sewing Row 2 "Top of the Tree"

1. Use the Diagonal Sewing Technique and sew **only** one background piece to the tree piece. Trim and press seam toward tree.

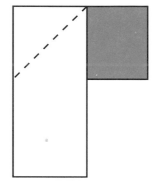

2. Add remaining background piece.

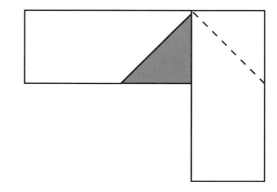

3. Trim and press seam toward tree.

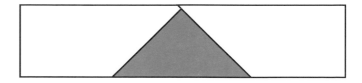

Sewing Rows

3 & 4 "Tree"

Use the Diagonal Sewing Technique to sew both rows. Trim and press seams toward tree.

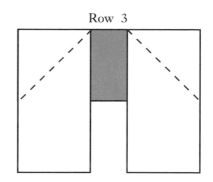

Row 3

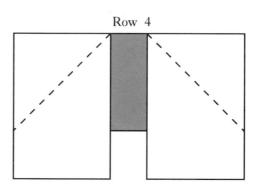

Row 4

Sewing Row 5

"Trunk"

Sew and press seams toward trunk.

Sewing the Rows

Together

Sew the six rows together matching the centers of each row. Press seams as shown.

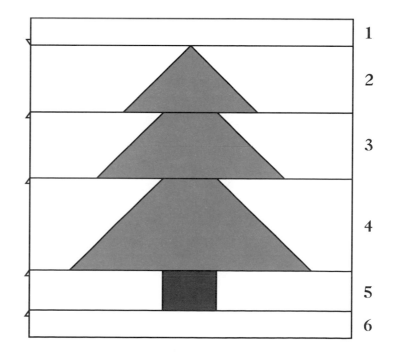

The Candle

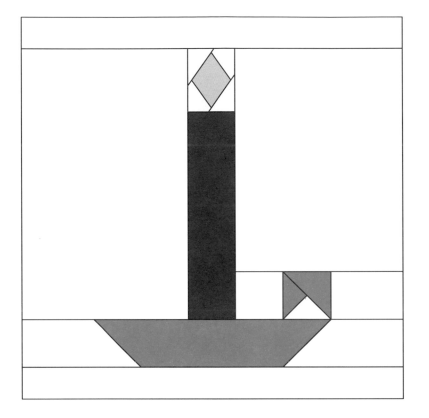

Cut from candle fabric:		
(1) 7" x 2"		2d

Cut from candleholder fabric:		
(1) 2" x 8"		3j
(1) 3" x 3"		2g

Cut from flame fabric:		
(1) 2 ½" x 2"		2c

Cut from background fabric:		
(1) 2 ½" x 45"--cut into:		
(2) 2 ½" x 13 ½"		1a,4a
(2) 2" x 4 ¾"		3i
(1) 2" x 3 ¼"		2h
(1) 2" x 2"		2f
(1) 9" x 6 ¼"		2b
(1) 7 ½" x 6 ¼"		2e
(		
1) 1 ¾" x 22" . . set aside to make flame		
(1) 3" x 3"		2g

Candles have glowed on important occasions for thousands of years. The Jews commemorated religious freedom by celebrating Hanukkah or Feast of Lights in December. Later the Christian world adopted this festive idea to celebrate the Nativity after Pope Gelasius established February 2, as Candlemas Day. This day honored the Virgin Mary 40 days after the birth of Christ when Joseph and Mary presented Jesus in the temple at Jerusalem where he was proclaimed "a light to lighten the Gentiles." (Luke 2:32) Candles are an integral part of the modern celebration of Christmas. They have come to symbolize the Star of Bethlehem, a sign of welcome to strangers, and Jesus as the "Light of the World."

❏ Layout Diagram

The 1 ¾" x 22" background strip is not shown in this diagram but is used to make the flame.
The 3" squares are layered in the diagram.

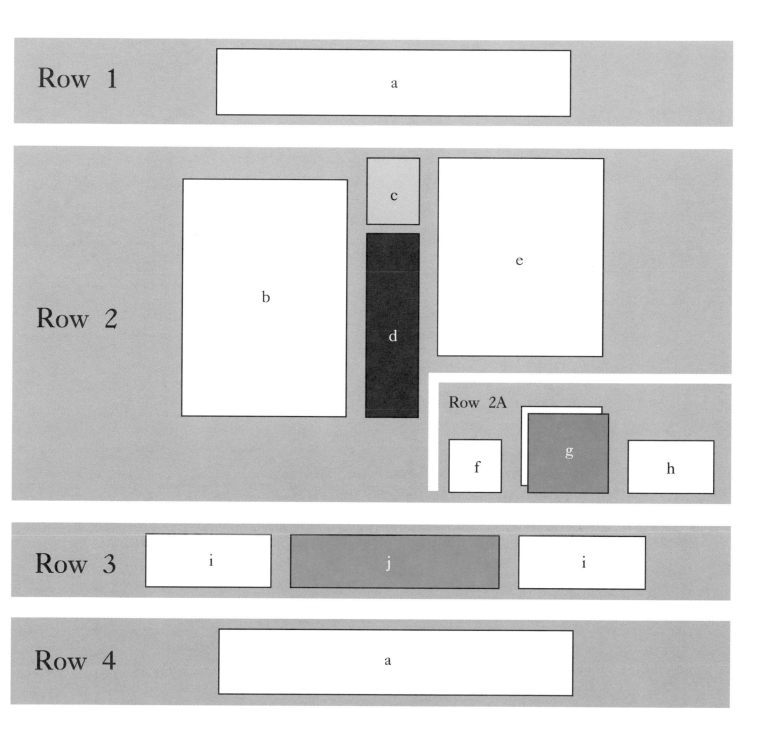

Sewing the Candle Block

Sewing Row 2 "Flame"

1. On the right side of flame (c), mark the center of each side. Draw connecting diagonal lines.

2. Cut the 1 ¾" x 22" background strip into 4 equal pieces.

3. Lay the first piece covering flame with right edge along right diagonal line. Sew.

4. Repeat on opposite diagonal line.

5. Trim flame and press seams toward flame.

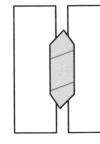

Sewn & folded back

6. Repeat for remaining diagonals. Trim and press seams toward flame.

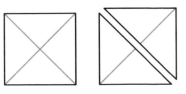

Sewn & folded back

7. Square flame to 2 ½" x 2".

Lay flame on point. Place the 1" ruler line down the center and trim right edge. Give flame a half turn, replace ruler and trim opposite side. Repeat for remaining two sides using 1 ¼" for the center line.

Flame may be smaller than shown.

Sewing Row 2A "Handle"

1. Draw diagonal lines on the wrong side of the background square (g). Place right sides together to the candleholder square (g). Cut on one diagonal.

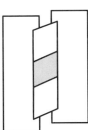

Discard the background triangle from the right half. Set aside the candleholder triangle until step 3.

2. With left half, sew on the line. Trim and press seam toward candleholder.

3. Sew the two triangles. Press seam toward one color triangle.

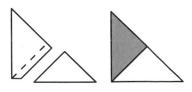

4. Square handle to 2"x 2".

   Lay the 45° ruler line along the diagonal line of the handle with the 1" ruler point on the center. Trim side and top. Give square a half turn, replace ruler and trim remaining two sides.

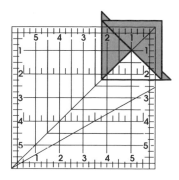

5. Add background pieces (f,h). Press seams away from handle.

Sewing Row 2 Together

1. Sew the flame to candle. Press seam down.

2. Sew handle to background piece (e). Press seam up.

3. Sew the vertical seams of Row 2. Press seams away from candle.

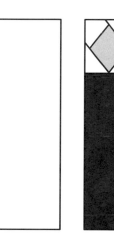

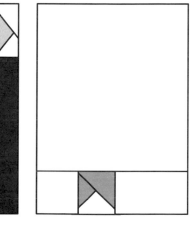

Sewing Row 3 "Candleholder"

Use the Diagonal Sewing Technique. Trim and press seams toward candleholder.

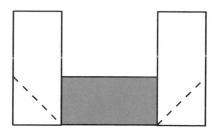

Sewing the Rows Together

1. Use the Stabilizing Pin Technique to match the outside handle seam to the diagonal candleholder seam. Sew. Press seam down.

2. Add Rows 1 and 4. Press seams as shown.

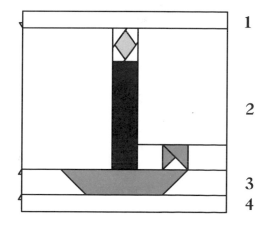

1

2

3

4

The Joy Block

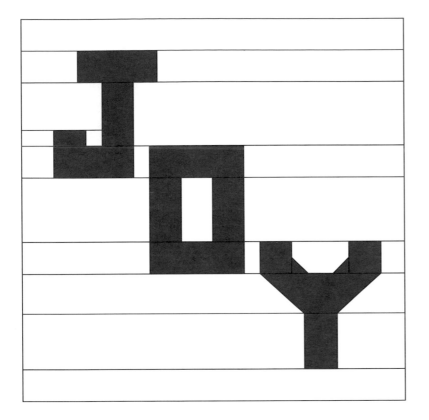

Cut from joy fabric:

(1) 1 1/2" x 45"--cut into:
- (2) 1 ½" x 3" 2c,4c
- (3) 1 ½" x 2 ½" 3f,5f
- (1) 1" x 1 ½" 3i
- (2) 1 ½" x 3 ½" 4m,6m
- (2) 1 ½" x 1 ½" 6s
- (2) 1" x 1" 6t
- (1) 2 ¼" x 1 ½" 8y

(1) 1 ¾" x 4" 7v

Cut from the background fabric:

(2) 2 ½" x 45"--cut into:
- (2) 2 ½" x 13 ½" 1a,9a
- (1) 2 ½" x 9 ½" 3g
- (1) 2 ½" x 6" 5q
- (1) 2 ½" x 5" 5o
- (1) 2 ½" x 1 ½" 5p
- (1) 2 ¼" x 9 ¾" 8x
- (1) 2 ¼" x 3 ¼" 8z
- (1) 2" x 3 ½" 3e
- (1) 1 ¾" x 9 ¾" 7u
- (1) 1 ¾" x 3 ¼" 7w

(1) 1 ½" x 45"--cut into:
- (2) 1" x 1 ½" 4l,6l
- (3) 1 ½" x 2" 4k,6k
- (1) 1 ½" x 8 ¾" 2d
- (1) 1 ½" x 5" 6r
- (1) 1 ½" x 6" 4n
- (1) 1 ½" x 2 ¾" 2b
- (1) 1" x 2" 3h
- (1) 1" x 1" 3j

The Christmas Season is filled with Joy! We sing "Joy to the World, the Lord is come." The Bible in Psalm 98 says, "Shout for joy to the Lord, all the Earth." Memories are filled with joyful times we've spent with family and friends. We share our joy during the season baking goodies, entertaining friends and neighbors, donating to the less fortunate, and caroling. Joy is what is in our hearts.

❏ Layout Diagram

Lay the cut pieces as shown in this diagram:

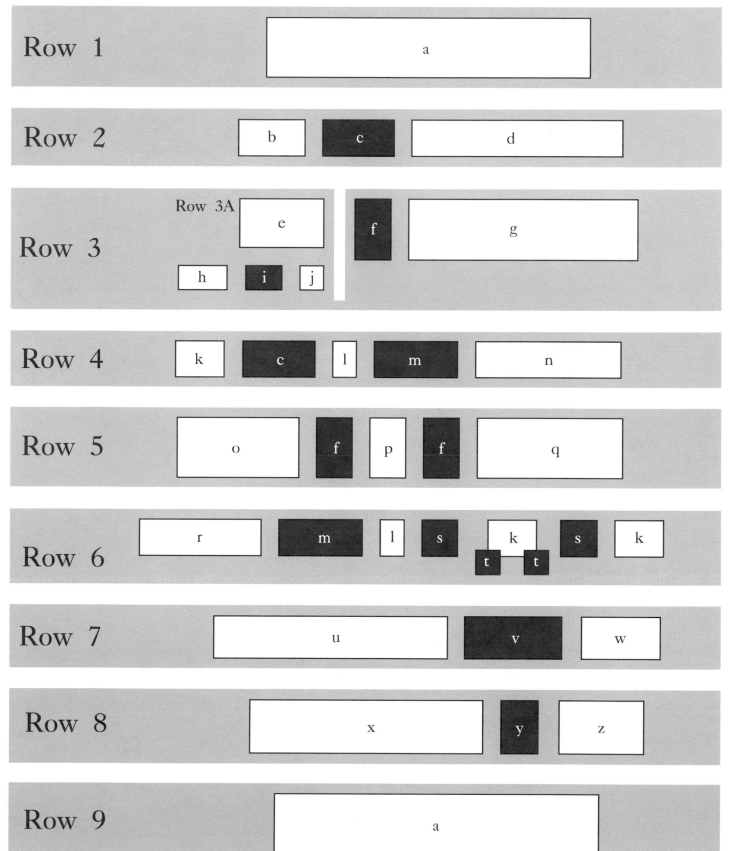

Sewing the Joy Block

Sewing Row 2
"Top of J"
Sew and press seams toward letter.

Sewing Row 3A
"Hook of J"
1. Sew the two background pieces (h,j) to the letter piece. Press seams toward background.

2. Sew the background piece (e) to the top. Press seam up.

Sewing Row 3
"Middle of J"
Sew and press seams toward background.

Sewing Row 4
"Bottom of J, Top of O"
Sew and press seams toward letters.

Sewing Row 5
"Middle of O"
Sew and press seams toward background.

20

Sewing Row 6
"Bottom of O,
Top of Y"

1. Use the Diagonal Sewing Technique to sew the two letter squares (t) to the bottom of the background piece (k). Trim and press seams toward letter.

2. Sew and press seams toward letters.

Sewing Row 7
"Middle of Y"

Use the Diagonal Sewing Technique. Trim and press seams toward letter.

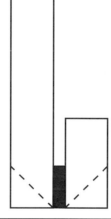

Sewing Row 8
"Tail of Y"

Sew and press seams toward letter.

Sewing the Rows
Together

1. Lock and sew the straight seams. Use Stabilizing Pin Technique to match diagonal seams.

2. Press seams as shown.

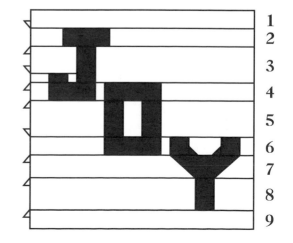

The Bell

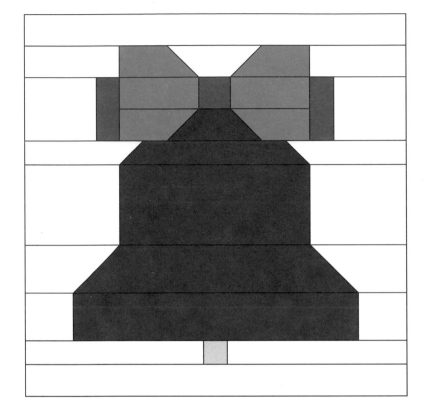

✄ Cutting Instructions

Cut from bell striker fabric:	
(1) 1 ¼" x 1 ¼"	7r

Cut from bell fabric:	
(1) 3" x 45"--cut into:	
(2) 2" x 9 ½"	5n,6p
(1) 3" x 6 ½"	4l
(1) 1 ¼" x 6 ½"	3j
(1) 1 ½" x 3 ½"	2h

Cut from dark bow fabric:	
(1) 1 ½" x 1 ½"	2e
(2) 2 ½" x 1 ¼"	2g

Cut from medium bow fabric:	
(1) 1 ½" x 22"--cut into:	
(6) 1 ½" x 3 ¼"	2c

Cut from the background fabric:	
(1) 2 ½" x 45"--cut into:	
(2) 2 ½" x 13 ½"	1a,8a
(2) 2 ½" x 3 ¼"	2f
(2) 2" x 2 ½"	6o
(1) 1 ½" x 45"--cut into:	
(2) 1 ½" x 4"	2b
(2) 1 ¼" x 4 ¾"	3i
(2) 1 ¼" x 6 ¾"	7q
(1) 1 ½" x 3 ½"	2d
(2) 2" x 4"	5m
(2) 3" x 4"	4k

I t has long been a Christmas custom that bells and chimes be sounded on Christmas Day. In England, there is an old legend of a Christmas Eve earthquake that buried a church, bells and all, deep in the ground. Yet the catastrophe was powerless to prevent the bells from being heard every Christmas thereafter. In our own country, one of the most popular poets of all time, Henry Wadsworth Longfellow, expressed the significance of this custom in his poem of 1863, "Christmas Bells":

I heard the bells on Christmas Day
Their old, familiar carols play,
And wild and sweet
The words repeat
Of peace on earth, good-will to men!

❒ Layout Diagram

Lay the cut pieces as shown in this diagram:

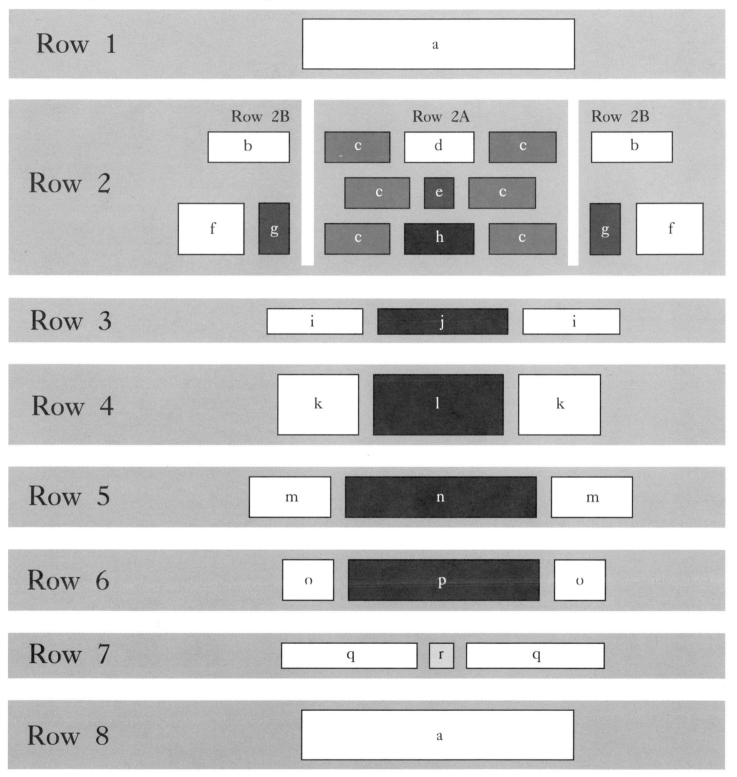

Row 1 — a

Row 2

Row 2B — b, f, g
Row 2A — c, d, c, c, e, c, c, h, c
Row 2B — b, g, f

Row 3 — i, j, i

Row 4 — k, l, k

Row 5 — m, n, m

Row 6 — o, p, o

Row 7 — q, r, q

Row 8 — a

Sewing the Bell Block

Sewing Row 2A
"Bow"

1. Use the Diagonal Sewing Technique to sew the top and bottom rows of Row 2A. Press seams toward bow.

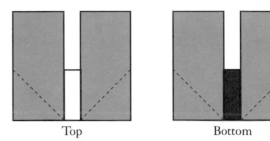

Top   Bottom

2. Sew the the middle row of 2A. Press seams toward center.

3. Use the Stabilizing Pin Technique to pin the three small rows of Row 2A. Sew and press seams toward center.

4. Square bow section to 3 ½" x 6 ½".

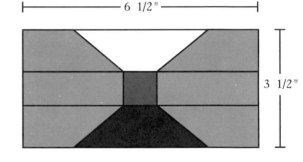

Sewing Row 2B
"Bow"

Sew the two opposite sections of Row 2B. Press the first seams toward the bow. Press the second seams toward the background.

Sewing Row 2
Together

Sew the 2B sections to the 2A section. Press seams away from center.

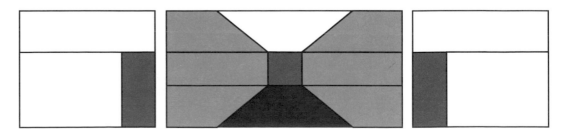

Sewing Rows
3 & 5 "Bell"

Use the Diagonal Sewing Technique to sew both rows. Trim and press seams toward bell.

Sewing Rows
4 & 6 "Bell"

Sew and press seams toward bell.

Sewing Row 7
"Bell Striker"

Sew and press seams toward bell striker.

Sewing the Rows
Together

1. Mark the center of each row.

2. Sew the rows by matching the centers and using the Stabilizing Pin Technique to match straight bell seams to diagonal bell seams.

3. Press seams as shown.

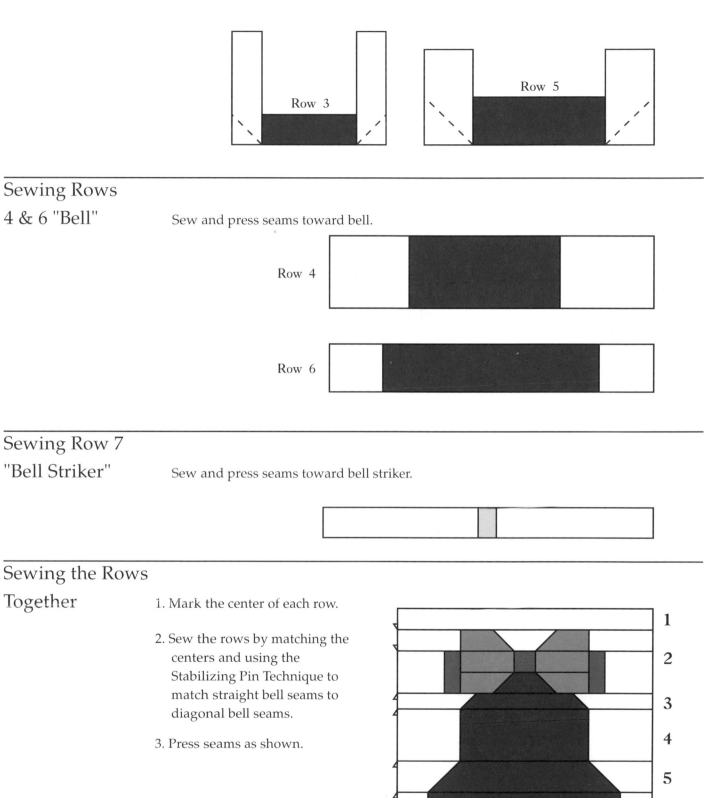

The Star of Bethlehem

✂ Cutting Instructions

Cut from star fabric:		
(8) 3" x 3"	. . . .	2c,3c,4c

Cut from 9-patch fabric:		
(4) 1 ¾" x 1 ¾"	. . . .	3f
(1) 3" x 3"	. . . .	3h

Cut from the background fabric:		
(1) 3" x 45"--cut into:		
(2) 3" x 5 ½"	. . . .	2d,4d
(4) 3" x 4 ½"	. . . .	2b,4b
(4) 3" x 1 ¾"	. . . .	3g
(1) 2 ½" x 45"--cut into:		
(2) 2 ½" x 13 ½"	. . . .	1a,5a
(2) 5 ½" x 4 ½"	. . . .	3e

After the Wisemen heard the king, they went on their way, and the star they saw in the East went ahead of them until it stopped over the place where the Child was. When they saw the star, they were overjoyed. On coming to the house, they saw the Child with his mother Mary, and they bowed down and worshiped him. (Matthew 2:9-11) The celebration of Christmas began when a star rose in the East and a Savior was born. That star has come to be known as the Star of Bethlehem. There are several different quilt blocks representing the Star of Bethlehem. This block is one of the adaptations.

❏ Layout Diagram

Lay the cut pieces as shown in this diagram:

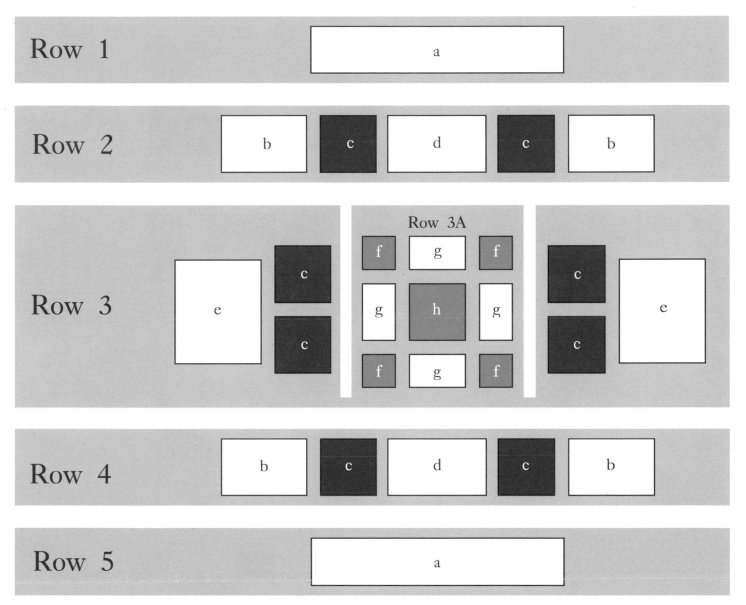

Sewing the Star Block

Sewing Rows
2 & 4 "Star Points"

1. Use the Diagonal Sewing Technique to sew a star square (c) to one end of **each** background piece (2d,4d). Trim and press seams toward star.

2. Repeat for opposite end of rectangles.

3. Sew the remaining background pieces of **each** row to the star points. Press seams toward background.

Sewing Row 3A
"9-Patch Center"

1. Sew the three small rows of the 9-patch square. Press seams toward 9-patch fabric.

2. Lock and pin the seams of each row. Sew. Press seams toward 9-patch center.

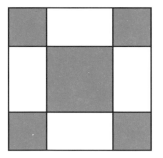

28

Sewing Row 3
"Star Points"

1. Use the Diagonal Sewing Technique to sew a star square (c) in the top right corner of each background piece (e). Trim and press seams toward star.

2. Repeat for bottom right corner of each background piece.

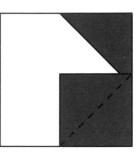

Sewing Row 3
Together

With star points on top, sew the two vertical seams. Press seams toward 9-patch.

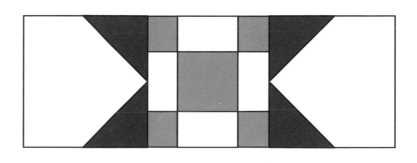

Sewing the Rows
Together

1. Lock and pin the four star corners to the 9-patch corners. With star points on top, sew Rows 2 and 4 to Row 3.

2. With star points on top, add Rows 1 and 5.

3. Press seams as shown.

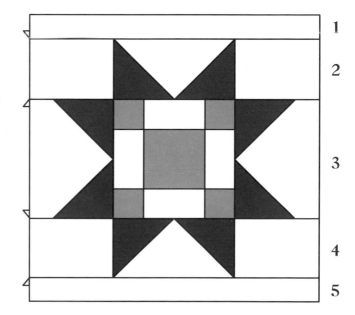

The Ornament

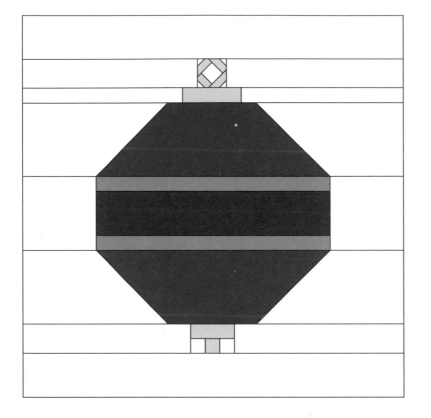

✄ Cutting Instructions

Cut from top cap and loop fabric:
(1) 1" x 2 ½" 3e
(1) ¾" x 9" . . set aside to make loop

Cut from ornament fabric:
(2) 3" x 8 ½" 4g,6g

Cut from center border fabric:
(2) 1" x 8 ½" 5i

Cut from decorative center fabric:
(1) 2" x 8 ½" 5j

Cut from bottom point fabric:
(1) 1" x 2" 7l
(1) 1" x 1" 7n

Cut from the background fabric:
(1) 3" x 45"--cut into:
    (2) 3" x 3" 5h
    (4) 3" x 5 ½" 4f,6f
    (2) 1 ½" x 6 ¼" 7k
    (3) 1" x 1" 2c,7m
(1) 2 ½" x 45"--cut into:
    (2) 2 ½" x 13 ½" 1a,8a
    (2) 1 ½" x 6 ½" 2b
(2) 1" x 6" 3d
(1) ¾" x 9" . . . set aside to make loop

From a legend told by G. Jacob, tenth-century geographer: "Every tree throughout the world bloomed and bore fruit on Christmas Eve; nature silently, but brilliantly, celebrated the Birth of Christ."

Tree ornaments continue this celebration by proclaiming our joy at Christ's birth. The custom of decorating evergreens with prized ornaments came to America with German immigrants in the 1700's. The custom slowly caught on, because unlike the Germans who bought their ornaments from shops in Germany, Americans hand-made their ornaments from cookies, candies, straw, wood and scraps of paper and fabric. In 1880, F. W. Woolworth displayed a few glass ornaments in his store and they sold immediately. Today most Christmas trees are loaded with sentimental ornaments that are elaborate or simple, and saved from year to year as family treasures.

❏ Layout Diagram

Lay the cut pieces as shown in the diagram:
A ¾" x 9" strip of both background and loop are not shown in this diagram, but will be used to make the loop of the ornament.

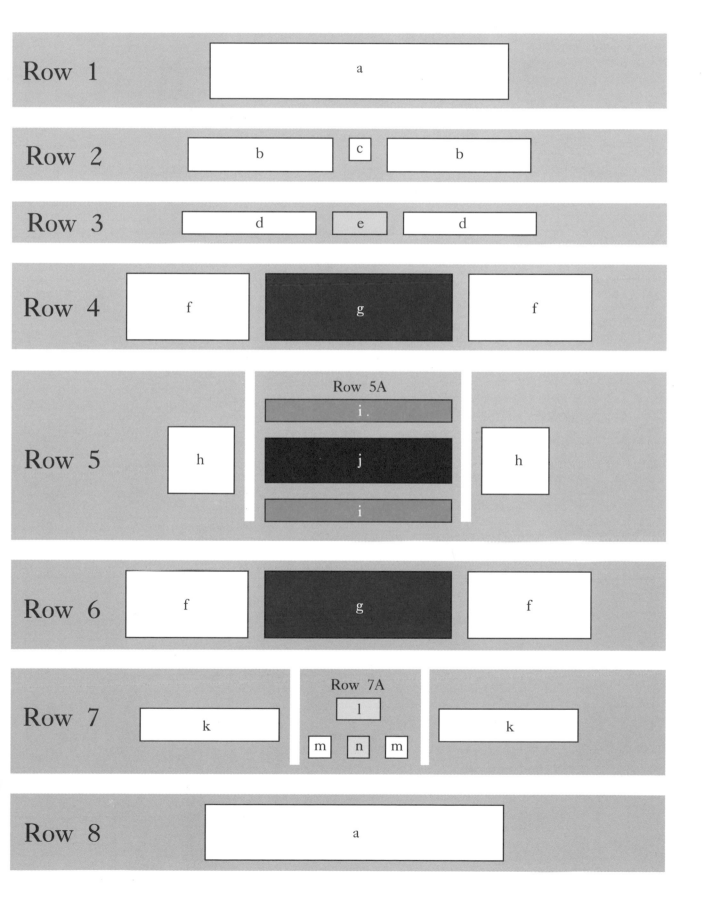

Sewing the Ornament Block

Sewing Row 2
"Loop"

1. Sew the ¾" x 9" loop strip to one edge of the background square (c). Trim ends even. Press seam away from center. Repeat for remaining three sides.

2. Repeat step 1 with the ¾" x 9" background strip.

3. Square loop to 1 ½" x 1 ½".

   Lay the loop on point. Place the ¾" ruler line down the center and trim right edge. Give loop a half turn, replace ruler and trim opposite side. Repeat for remaining two edges.

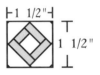

4. Add the background pieces. Press seams toward background.

Sewing Row 3
"Top Cap"

Sew and press seams toward top cap.

Sewing Rows
4 & 6 "Ornament"

Use the Diagonal Sewing Technique to sew Rows 4 and 6. Trim and press seams toward ornament.

When finished, turn one row around.

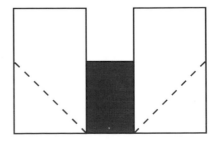

Sewing Row 5
"Decorative Center"

1. Sew the three pieces of Row 5A. Press seams toward decorative center.

2. Add the background pieces. Press seams toward background.

Sewing Row 7
"Bottom Point"

1. Sew the three small pieces of Row 7A. Press seams toward center.

2. Sew the point piece to the top. Press seam up.

3. Add the background pieces. Press seams toward background.

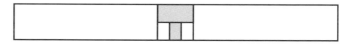

Sewing the Rows Together

1. Mark the center of each row.

2. Sew the rows by matching the centers and use the Stabilizing Pin Technique to match straight seams to diagonal seams.

3. Press seams as shown.

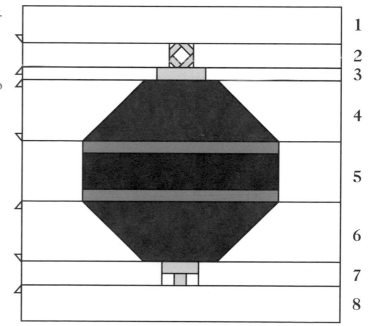

The Stocking

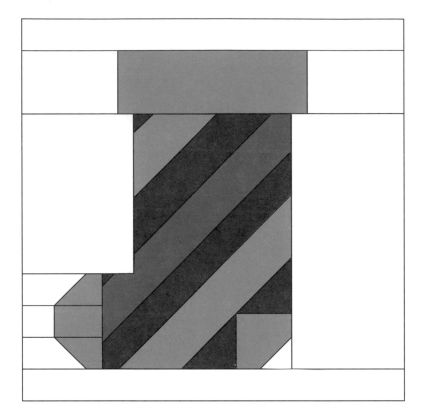

✂ Cutting Instructions

Cut for the stocking:

(2) 2 ¼" x 2 ¼" 3i
(3) 1 ½" x 14" strips of various fabrics
(3) 2" x 14" strips of various fabrics

Cut from cuff, heel, and toe fabric:

(1) 2 ½" x 6 ½" (cuff) 2c
(1) 2 ¼" x 2 ¼" (heel) 3j
(3) 1 ½" x 2" (toe) 3g

Cut from the background fabric:

(1) 2 ½" x 45"--cut into:
    (2) 2 ½" x 13 ½" 1a,4a
    (2) 2 ½" x 4" 2b
    (2) 1 ½" x 3" 3f
(1) 4 ½" x 22"--cut into:
    (1) 8 ½" x 4 ½" 3e
    (1) 5 ½" x 4 ½" 3d
    (1) 1 ½" x 2" 3h
    (1) 1 ½" x 1 ½" 3k

Clement C. Moore penned these famous words long ago on a Christmas in 1822. "The stockings were hung by the chimney with care, in hopes that St. Nicholas soon would be there."

In those days, Christmas trees were not readily available so children hung empty stockings on the fireplace before bedtime. They slept with great anticipation of Santa's arrival and the gifts he would bring. Those stockings were well-worn, everyday apparel--far different from the large, personalized Christmas stockings hung by children today. However, after almost two centuries, the stocking has retained its original purpose--to be gleefully retrieved at the crack of dawn on Christmas morning, bulging with Santa's bounty.

❏ Layout Diagram

Lay the cut pieces as shown in this diagram:

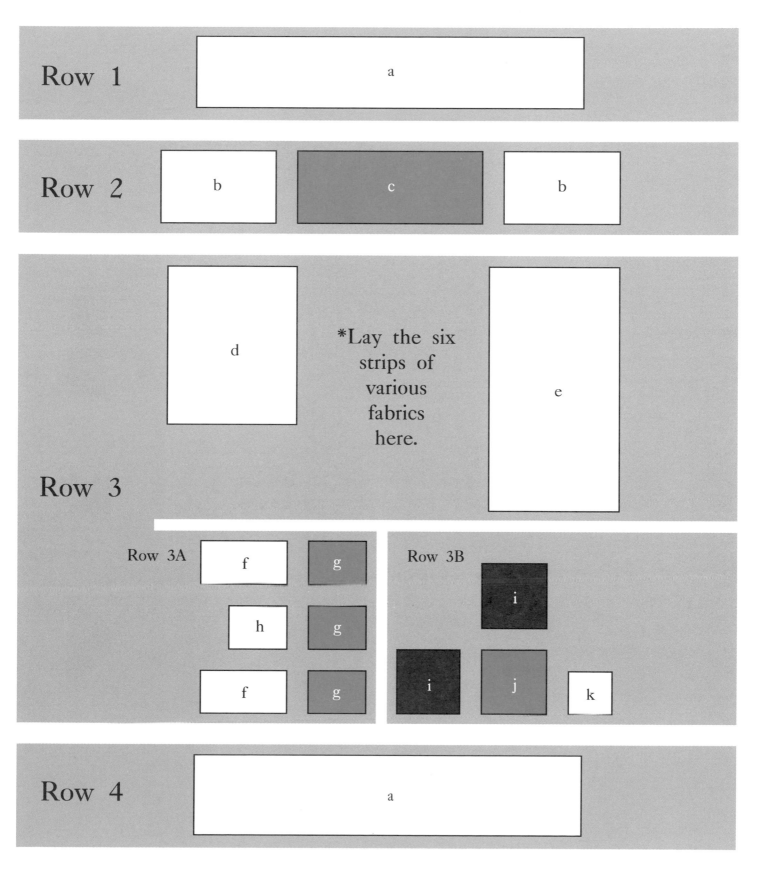

Row 1

a

Row 2

b

c

b

Row 3

d

*Lay the six strips of various fabrics here.

e

Row 3A

f

g

h

g

f

g

Row 3B

i

i

j

k

Row 4

a

Sewing the Stocking Block

Sewing Row 2
"Cuff"

Sew and press seams toward cuff.

Sewing Row 3A

"Toe"

1. Use the Diagonal Sewing Technique to sew the two small outside rows of Row 3A. Trim and press seams toward toe.

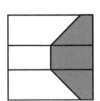

2. Sew the middle small row. Press seam toward toe.

3. Use the Stabilizing Pin Technique to pin the three rows. Sew. Press seams toward center.

Sewing Row 3B
"Heel"

1. Use the Diagonal Sewing Technique to sew the background square (k) in the bottom right corner of the heel square (j). Trim and press seam toward heel.

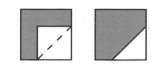

2. Sew a stocking square (i) to the top of heel. Press seam away from heel.

3. Sew a stocking square (i) to the left side of the heel. Press seam away from heel.

   Square heel if necessary.

4. Place the 45° ruler line along the bottom edge of the heel, creating a diagonal line along the stocking squares, ¼" from the heel. Trim along the diagonal.

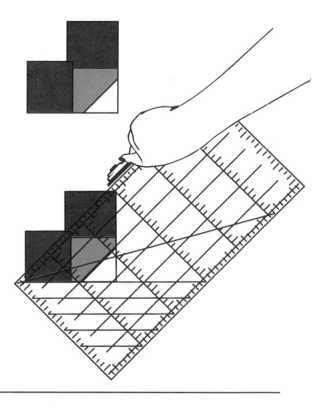

Sewing Row 3
"Stripped Stocking Section"

1. Sew the six stocking strips together. Press seams all in one direction.

2. Sew the heel section to the center of the stripped stocking section. Press seam away from heel.

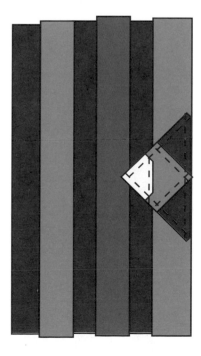

Drawing the Stocking Section

1. Study the diagram. Draw the five sides of the stocking on the stripped stocking section.

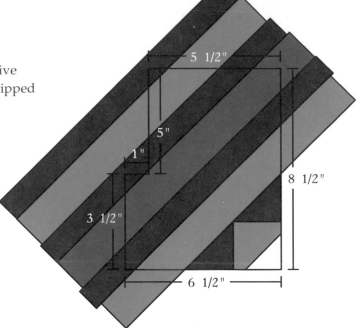

2. Carefully cut out the stocking.

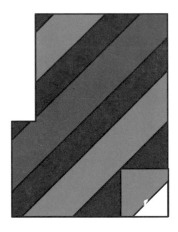

Sewing the Stocking Section

1. Sew the background piece (e) to the right side of stocking. Press seam toward background.

2. Sew the toe section to the 3 ½" side of stocking. Press seam toward stocking.

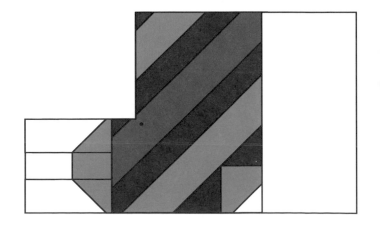

3. Make a dot on the **right** side of the stocking section ¼" from the inside corner.

4. Make a dot on the **wrong** side of the background piece (d) ¼" from the bottom left corner.

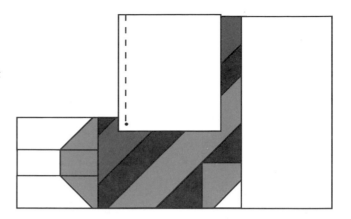

5. Lay the background piece, right sides together, to the stocking. Match and pin the **dot** on the background to the **dot** on the stocking. Backstitch and sew from the dot to the top edge.

6. Carefully clip the seam diagonally to the sewn point.

7. Fold the top edge down, and pin the bottom edge of the background piece to the top edge of the toe. Carefully sew from the outside edges to the dot and backstitch.

Stitches never touch at the dot.

8. Press seams toward background.

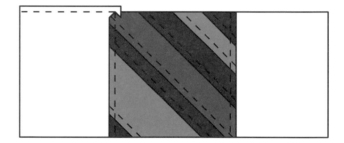

Sewing the Rows Together

1. Center and sew Row 2 to Row 3.

2. Add Rows 1 and 4.

3. Press seams as shown.

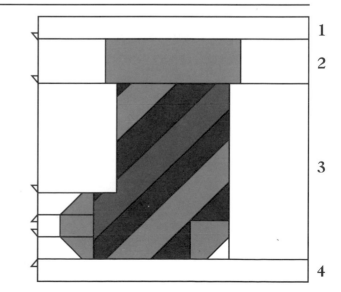

The Home Block

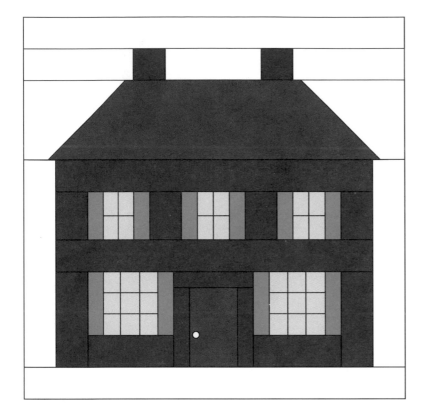

✂ Cutting Instructions

Cut from house fabric:

(1) 1 ½" x 45"--cut into:
      (2) 1 ½" x 3 ¼" 4q
      (2) 1 ½" x 10 ½" 4g
      (2) 3 ½" x 1 ½" 4m
      (3) 3" x 1" 4l
(4) 2" x 1 ½" 4h

Cut from roof fabric:

(1) 3" x 10 ½" 3f

Cut from chimney fabric:

(2) 1 ½" x 1 ½" 2c

Cut from shutter fabric:

(4) 2 ½" x 1" 4n
(6) 2" x 1" 4i

Cut from door fabric:

(1) 3" x 2" 4p

Cut from window fabric:

(2) 2 ½" x 2 ¼" 4o
(3) 2" x 1 ½" 4j

Cut from the background fabric:

(1) 2 ½" x 45"--cut into:
      (2) 2 ½" x 13 ½" 1a,5a
      (2) 7" x 2 ¼" 4k
(1) 3" x 22"--cut into:
      (2) 3" x 4 ½" 3e
      (2) 1 ½" x 4 ¾" 2b
      (1) 1 ½" x 3" 2d

Home for Christmas! Every year we hear this phrase over and over again. It's the one holiday we all try to celebrate at home. And rightly so, for the original event on a cold desert night of beautiful stars was a family affair. Since then, Christmas has always been celebrated as a family, with special traditions belonging to each household but familiar to families everywhere. Thinking of home at Christmas time brings memories of delicious smells, brightly decorated trees, the rush to finish last minute gifts, mounds of presents, crisp night air filled with colored lights and Christmas carols floating through the room, and oh! so much more.....

❏ Layout Diagram

Lay the cut pieces as shown in this diagram:

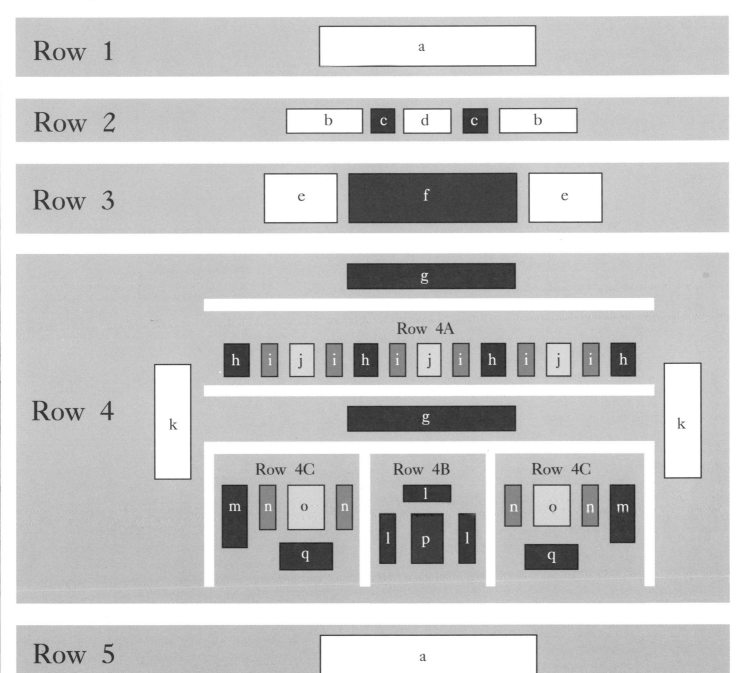

Sewing the Home Block

Sewing Row 2
"Chimneys"

Sew and press seams toward chimneys.

Sewing Row 3
"Roof"

Use the Diagonal Sewing Technique. Trim and press seams toward roof.

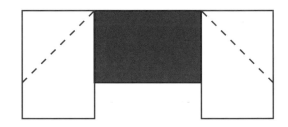

Sewing Row 4A
"Second Floor Windows"

1. Assembly-line sew a shutter (i) to both long sides of each window (j). Press seams toward shutters.

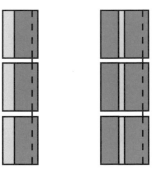

2. Sew the house and window sections of Row 4A together. Press seams toward shutters.

   Sliver trim long edges if uneven.

Sewing Row 4B
"Door"

1. Sew a house piece (l) to each side of the door. Press seams toward door.

2. Sew a house piece (l) to the top of the door section. Press seam toward house.

Sewing Row 4C
"First Floor Windows"

1. Sew a shutter (n) to each side of the windows (o). Press seams toward shutters.

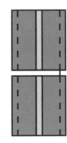

2. Sew a house piece (q) to the bottom of each large window section. Press seams toward house.

3. Sew a house piece (m) to the **opposite** edge of each window section. Press seams toward house.

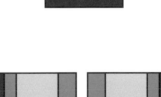

4. Sew the first floor door and windows together. Press seams towards door.

Sliver trim long edges if uneven.

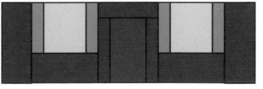

Sewing Row 4 Together

Outside edges of Row 4 may not match up, but will be trimmed later.

1. Center and sew a long house piece (g) to the top of each window section. Press seams toward house.

2. Line up the windows of each floor and sew the two floors together. Press seam toward house.

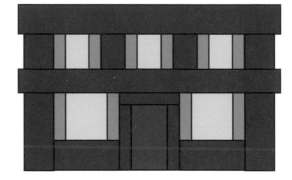

3. To trim the outside edges , place the 5" ruler line down the center of the door. Trim along right edge.

4. Give block a half turn, and repeat for the opposite side.

   The house should measure 10" wide.

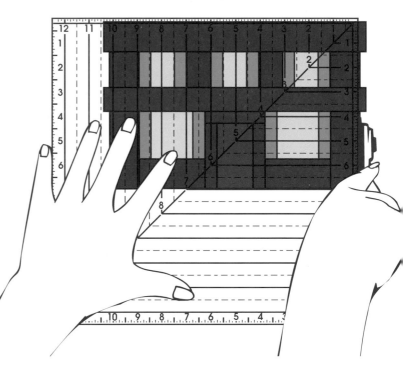

5. Sew a background piece to each side of house. Press seams toward background.

   Sliver trim top and bottom edges even with house.

Windows Panes and Doorknob

1. Draw lines for the window panes. Stitch with the sewing machine or hand embroider.

2. Zigzag or hand embroider a doorknob on the front door.

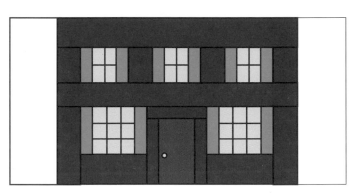

Sewing the Rows Together

1. Sew the rows by matching the centers.

   Roof overhang is approximately ¼". Chimneys are inset ¼".

2. Press seams as shown.

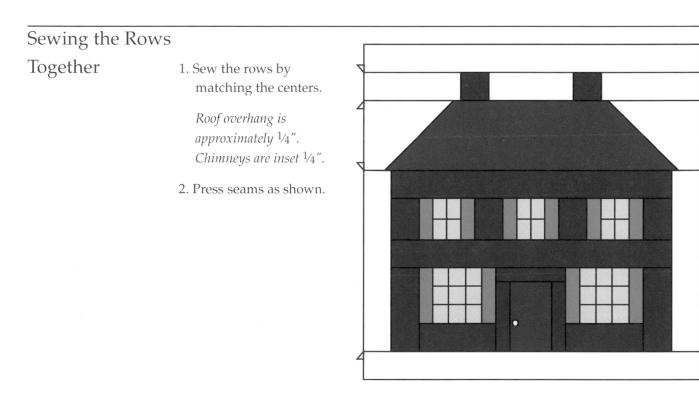

The Church

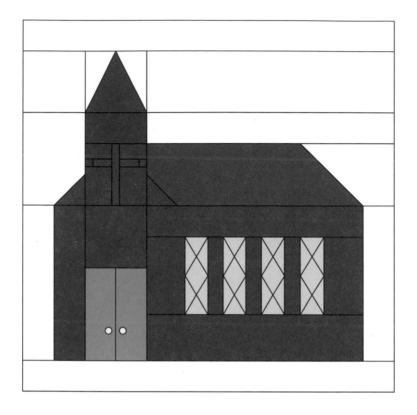

Cross Section:

These pieces will be cut later.

Cut from church fabric:

(1) 3" x 45"--cut into:
- (2) 3" x 1 ¾" 4p
- (3) 3" x 1" 4r
- (2) 1 ½" x 1 ½" 3f
- (1) 2 ½" x 2 ½" 4m
- (1) 2" x 7 ½" 4s
- (1) 1 ½" x 7 ½" 4n
- (1) 1 ½" x 5 ½" 4l
- (1) 1 ½" x 2 ½" 3g
- (1) 2 ½" x 2 ½" Optional: cut if omitting cross

Cut from roof fabric:

(1) 2 ½" x 7 ½" 3i

Cut from window fabric:

(4) 3" x 1 ¼" 4q

Cut from door fabric:

(2) 3 ½" x 1 ½" 4o

Cut from steeple fabric:

(1) 3" x 3" 2c

Cut from the background fabric:

(1) 2 ½" x 45"--cut into:
- (2) 2 ½" x 13 ½" 1a,5a
- (1) 2 ½" x 4" 3j
- (1) 2 ½" x 9" 2d
- (1) 2 ½" x 3" 2b

(1) 2" x 45"--cut into:
- (2) 2" x 5 ½" 4k
- (2) 2" x 6"--set aside to make steeple
- (1) 1 ½" x 9" 3h

(1) 3 ½" x 3" 3e

The first Christmas was a creative experience: God performed the unexpected. A baby was born in a rustic stable in Bethlehem. Angels sang, shepherds left their flocks, and Wise Men began their journey. The spirit of this first Christmas was joy, astonishment, and wonder. Two thousand years later, on December 24, the eve of Christ's birth, Christians around the world welcome Christmas with midnight worship in the church of their choice. Carols, prayers, and the pageantry of the Nativity, remind us of that first Christmas long ago.

☐ Layout Diagram

Lay the cut pieces as shown in this diagram:
(2) 2" x 6" strips of background fabric are not shown in layout but are used to make the steeple.

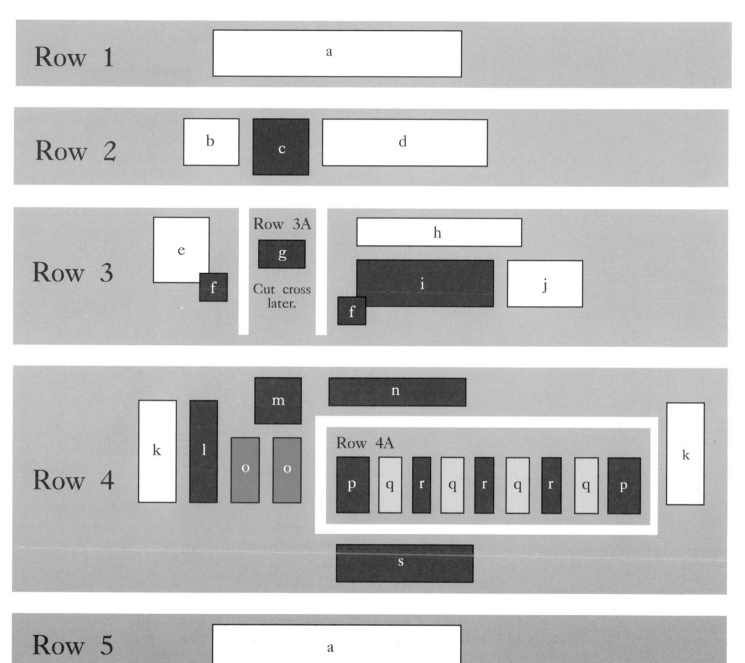

Sewing the Church Block

Sewing Row 2
"Steeple"

1. On the right side of steeple (c), draw a line
¼" from the bottom edge.

2. Mark the center point of the drawn line.
Mark 1" on either side of the center point.

3. At the center point, measure up 2" and mark.

4. Draw diagonal lines connecting the three
points to form a triangle.

5. Draw a second set of diagonal lines ¼"
outside the first diagonal lines.

6. Lay the right edge of a 2" x 6" background
strip, right sides together, along the right
outside diagonal line. Sew. Trim excess
steeple fabric. Press seam toward steeple.

7. Repeat for opposite diagonal.

Sewn & folded back

8. Square the steeple to 2 ½" x 2 ½".

    *Place the 1 ¼" ruler line down the center and
    trim right side. Give steeple a half turn, replace
    ruler, and trim opposite side. Trim bottom even
    with steeple. Measure up 2 ½", leaving a ¼"
    seam allowance at steeple point and trim.*

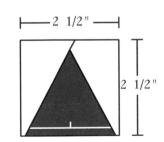

9. Add the two background pieces. Press
seams toward steeple.

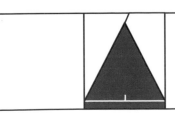

Cutting and Sewing Row 3A "Cross"

If omitting cross, skip to "Sewing Row 3 Roof."

Sew cross with scant ¼" seams.

Cut from cross fabric:
(1) ¾" x 2 ½"
(2) ¾" x 1"

Cut from church fabric:
(2) 1 ¾" x 1 ¾"
(2) ¾" x 1 ¼"
(2) 1" x 1 ¾"

1. Sew the ¾" x 1" cross pieces to the ¾" x 1 ¼" church pieces along the ¾" side. Press seams toward church.

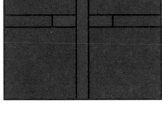

2. Sew the 1" x 1 ¾" church pieces to the top edges. Press seams toward church.

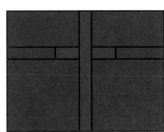

3. Sew the 1 ¾" church squares to the bottom edges. Press seams toward church.

4. Line up the horizontal seams and sew the side cross sections to the cross center. Press seams away from center.

5. Square the cross section to 2 ½" x 2 ½".

   Keep cross centered.

⊢——— 2 1/2" ———⊣

2 1/2"

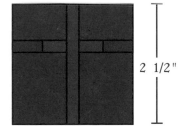

6. Sew the church piece (g) to the top of cross section. Press seam away from cross.

Sewing Row 3
"Roof"

1. Use the Diagonal Sewing Technique to sew the background piece (j) to the end of the roof piece (i). Trim and press seam toward roof.

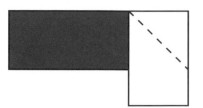

2. Use the Diagonal Sewing Technique to sew a church square (f) in the bottom left corner of the roof. Trim and press seam toward roof.

3. Sew the background strip (h) to the top of the roof. Press seam away from roof.

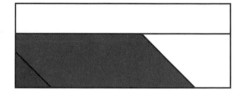

4. Use the Diagonal Sewing Technique to sew a church square (f) in the bottom right corner of the background piece (e). Trim and press seam toward church.

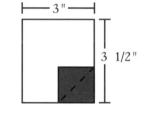

5. Sew Row 3. Press seams away from cross.

Sewing Row 4A
"Windows"

1. Sew and press seams toward windows.

2. Window section should measure 7 ½" long. If necessary, sliver trim keeping windows centered.

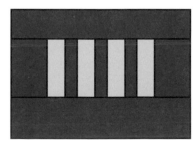

3. Sew church piece (n) to the top. Sew church piece (s) to the bottom. Press seams away from windows.

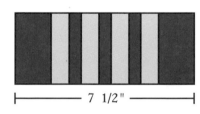

Sewing Row 4

1. Sew the door pieces (o) together. Press seam open.

2. Sew the church piece (m) above the doors. Press seam toward church.

3. Sew Row 4. Press seams toward door.

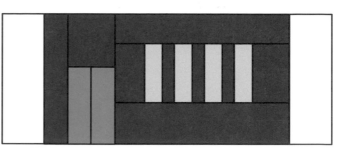

Window Panes and Doorknobs

1. Draw lines for window panes. Stitch with sewing machine or hand embroider.

2. Zigzag or hand embroider doorknobs on the front doors.

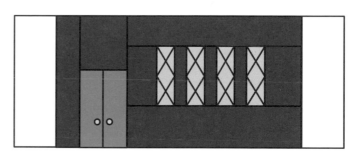

Sewing the Rows Together

1. Use the Stabilizing Pin Technique to match the roof seams of Row 3 to the church seams of Row 4. Sew. Press seam toward roof.

2. Match the diagonal seams of Row 2 to the straight seams of Row 3. Sew. Press seam toward steeple.

3. Add Rows 1 and 5. Press seams as shown.

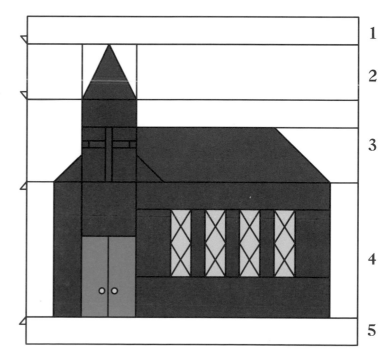

The Angel

There are no more delightful figures in the Christmas story than the heavenly host of angels. Throughout the Old and New Testaments, angels appear suddenly and act to man as messengers of God. They burst upon events with a joy that brings us closer to God and His awesome power and majesty.

"And, lo, the angel of the Lord came upon them, . . . And the angel said unto them, Fear not: for, behold, I bring you good tidings of great joy, which shall be to all people. For unto you is born this day in the city of David a Savior, which is Christ the Lord." (Luke, 2:8-14)

✂ Cutting Instructions

Cut from robe fabric:

(1) 3 ¼" x 22"--cut into:
(1) 3 ¼" x 3 ½"	. . . .	4s
(2) 3" x 1"	. . . .	4n
(2) 1" x 2"	. . . .	4j
(1) 2 ¼" x 1 ½"	. . . .	4q
(1) 1 ½" x 3 ½"	. . . .	3i

Cut from robe trim:

(2) 3" x 1"	. . . .	4o
(1) 1" x 3 ½"	. . . .	4t

Cut from wing fabric:

(1) 2 ¼" x 22"--cut into:
(2) 2 ¼" x 6 ¼"	. . . .	4m
(2) 1 ½" x 2 ¼"	. . . .	3f
(2) 1 ½" x 1 ½"	. . . .	3g

Cut from halo fabric:

(1) ⅞" x 8" . . . . set aside to make halo

Cut from hair fabric:

(1) 1" x 6" . . . . set aside to make hair

Cut from hands and face fabric:

(1) 1" x 1 ½"	. . . .	4k
(1) 1 ¼" x 1 ½"	. . . .	4p
(1) 2" x 2"	. . . .	2d

Cut from the background fabric:

(1) 3 ¾" x 45"--cut into:
(2) 3 ¾" x 6 ¾"	. . . .	4l
(2) 3 ¼" x 5 ½"	. . . .	2b
(2) 2 ¾" x 2 ¼"	. . . .	4r
(1) 3 ¾" x 3 ¾"	. . . .	2c

(1) 2 ½" x 45"--cut into:
(2) 2 ½" x 13 ½"	. . . .	1a,5a
(2) 1 ½" x 1 ½"	. . . .	3h
(2) 1 ½" x 4 ¾"	. . . .	3e

❏ Layout Diagram

Lay the cut pieces as shown in this diagram:
A $\frac{7}{8}$" x 8" halo strip and a 1" x 6" hair strip are not shown in this diagram but are used to make the head.

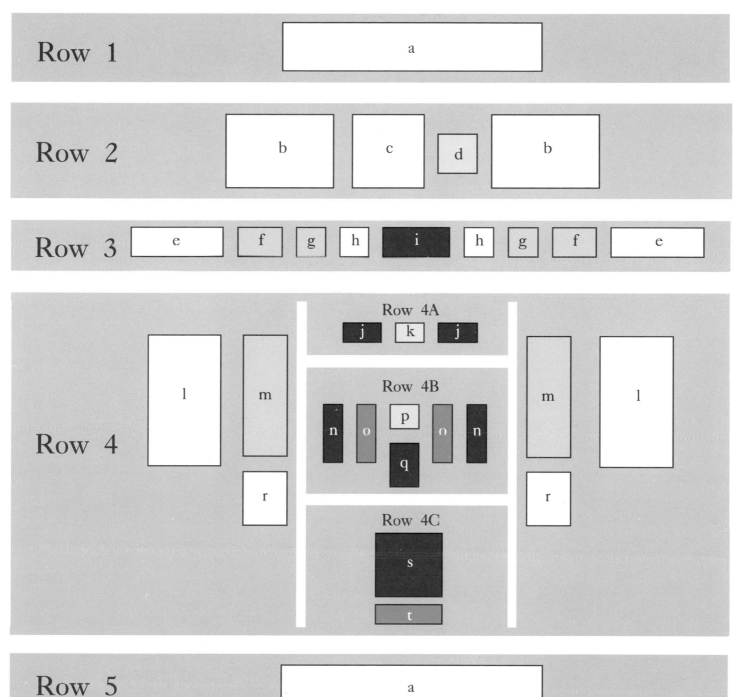

Sewing the Angel Block

Sewing Row 2
"Head"

1. Sew the strip of hair fabric to one side of the face square (d). Press seam toward hair. Trim ends even. Repeat for the next side of face.

2. Repeat with the halo strip. Trim ends even. Press seams toward halo.

3. Cut the background square (c) into 4 triangles.

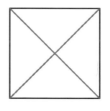

4. Center and sew triangles on opposite sides of the head. Press seams away from head.

5. Repeat for the remaining two sides.

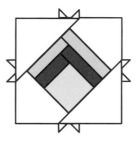

6. Square head piece to 3 ½" x 3 ¼".

   Place the 1 ¾" ruler line down the center and trim right edge. Give head a half turn, replace ruler, and trim opposite side. Trim at halo point. Measure down 3 ¼" to neck and trim.

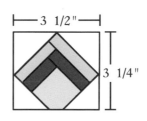

7. Add the background pieces (b). Press seams away from head.

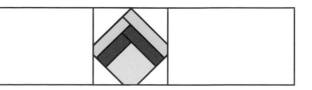

Sewing Row 3
"Top of Robe and
Top of Wings"

1. Place background squares (h), right sides together, to wing squares (g). Draw a diagonal line. Sew on the diagonal line. Trim and press seam toward wing.

2. Use the Diagonal Sewing Technique to sew the squares from step 1 to the ends of the robe piece (i). Trim and press seams toward robe. Set aside.

3. Use the Diagonal Sewing Technique to sew a wing piece (f) to **each** background piece (e). Trim and press seams toward wing.

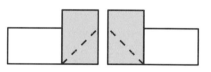

4. Sew the three sections of Row 3. Press seams toward center.

Sewing Row 4A
"Point of Hands"

Use the Diagonal Sewing Technique to sew one robe piece (j) to the hand piece (k). Trim and press seam toward robe before adding the remaining robe piece.

Sewing Row 4B
"Hands and
Sleeves"

1. Sew the hand piece (p) to the robe piece (q). Press seam toward robe.

2. Sew the robe trim pieces (o) to the robe sleeve pieces (n). Press seams toward robe sleeves.

3. Sew the hand and sleeve sections. Press seams toward sleeves.

Sewing Row 4C
"Robe Trim"

Sew and press seam toward trim.

Sewing Rows
4A, 4B, and 4C
Together

1. Use the Stabilizing Pin Technique and sew the hands point (4A) to the hand and sleeve section (4B). Press seam down.

2. Sew the completed hand section to the robe section (4C). Press seams down.

3. Sliver trim the sides to 3 ½" wide.

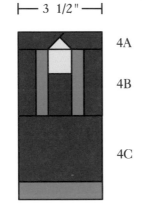

Sewing Row 4
"Wings"

Use the Diagonal Sewing Technique to sew a background piece (r) to each wing piece (m). Trim and press seams toward wings.

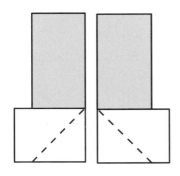

Sewing Row 4
Together

Match the five pieces at the **top** edges. Sew. Press seams away from the center.

Sliver trim bottom edges if uneven.

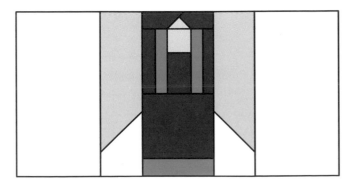

Sewing the Rows Together

1. Begin with Rows 3 and 4. Lock and pin the vertical seams. Use the Stabilizing Pin Technique to match the wing seams. Sew. Press seam whichever way it lies best.

2. Add Row 2. Lock and pin the head seams to the wing seams. Sew. Press seam up.

3. Add Rows 1 and 5. Press seams as shown.

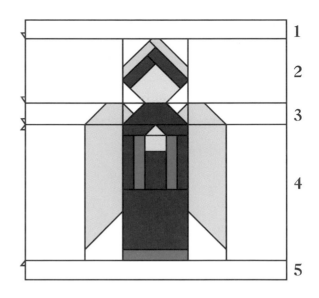

The Wreath

✂ Cutting Instructions

Cut from wreath fabric:

(1) 2 ¾" x 45"--cut into:
(2) 3" x 2 ¾"	2i
(2) 3 ½" x 1 ¾"	2e
(2) 1 ½" x 3 ¾"	2l
(1) 2 ¾" x 10"	3o
(1) 1 ¼" x 10"	2c

(9) 1 ½" x 1 ½" 2d

Cut from medium bow fabric:

(1) 1 ½" x 30" . . . set aside to make bow

Cut from dark bow fabric:

(2) 3" x 1 ½" 2k
(3) 1 ½" x 1 ½" 2f

Cut from the background fabric:

(1) 2 ¾" x 45"--cut into:
(2) 2 ¾" x 4 ½"	3n
(2) 2 ¾" x 2 ¾"	2b
(2) 2 ½" x 13 ½"	1a,4a

(1) 1 ½" x 22"--cut into:
(3) 3" x 1 ½"	2j
(3) 1 ½" x 1 ½"	2g
(1) 1 ½" x 5 ½"	2m

(2) 7 ¾" x 2 ¼" 2h

Although the tree may be the most spectacular decoration in our homes at Christmas time, it is by no means the only one. Decking the halls is an old tradition that stems from the belief that evergreens must have magical powers to thrive all year round. The Scandinavians brought the custom of hanging a wreath of fir or pine bough on the front door to America in 1638. Today the traditional wreath on the front door has become a gesture of friendship and welcome. Most often, a simple round of fresh evergreens topped by a big red bow greets visitors.

❏ Layout Diagram

Lay the cut pieces as shown in this diagram:
The 1 ½" x 30" medium bow strip is not shown in this diagram but is used to make the bows.

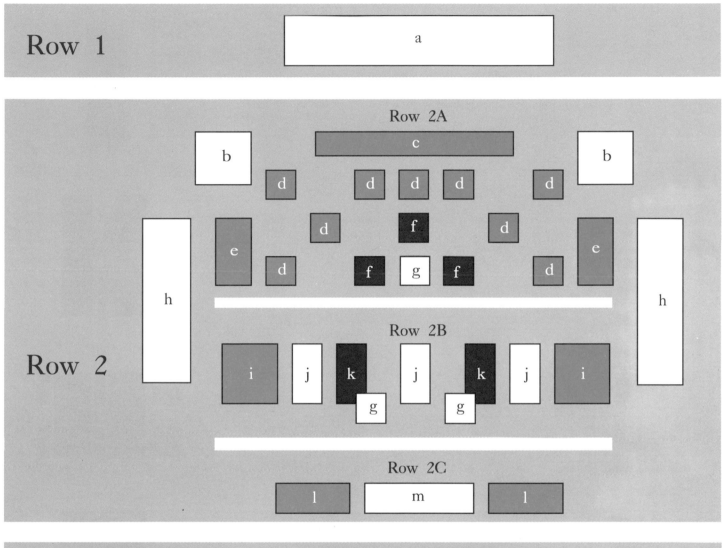

Sewing the Wreath

Sewing Row 2A
"Bow"

1. Cut the medium bow strip into six equal pieces.

2. Sew two center wreath squares (d), right sides together, to a medium bow piece.

3. Sew the opposite side of wreath squares to a second medium bow piece. Press seams toward bow.

4. Trim sides even with wreath squares.

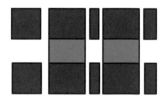

5. Sew a medium bow piece to each trimmed side. Press seams toward bow.

6. Turn bow and trim sides even. Bow squares should measure 3 ½".

Keep seams horizontal for the remaining steps.

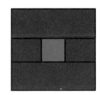

7. Use the Diagonal Sewing Technique to sew three wreath squares (d) and one dark bow square (f) on the corners of each bow section as shown.

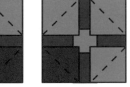

8. Trim and press seams away from bow.

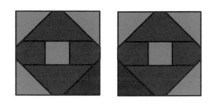

9. Sew the three knot squares (d, f, g). Press seams toward knot.

10. Use the Stabilizing Pin Technique to match the knot to the diagonal seams of the bow. Sew. Press seams toward knot.

11. Sew wreath pieces (e) to each side of bow section. Press seams toward wreath.

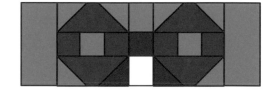

12. Sew wreath piece (c) to the top of the bow section. Press seams toward wreath.

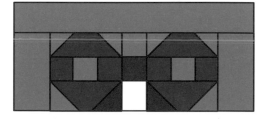

13. Use the Diagonal Sewing Technique to sew background squares (b) to the upper corners. Trim and press seams toward background.

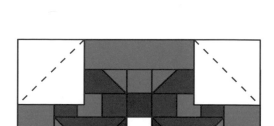

Sewing Row 2B "Middle of Wreath"

1. Use the Diagonal Sewing Technique to sew a background square (g) to each dark bow piece (k). Trim and press seams toward bow.

2. Sew Row 2B. Press seams as shown.

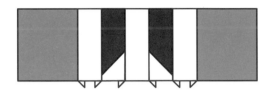

Sewing Row 2C "Bottom Curve of Wreath"

Use the Diagonal Sewing Technique. Trim and press seams toward wreath.

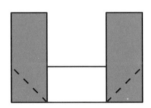

Sewing Row 2 Together

1. Use the Stabilizing Pin Technique to lock the six seams of Row 2A and Row 2B. Sew. Press seam down.

   If rows do not match correctly, make small adjustments, where necessary.

2. Use the Stabilizing Pin Technique to match the seams of Row 2B to Row 2C. Press seam down.

3. Add the background pieces (h). Press seams toward background.

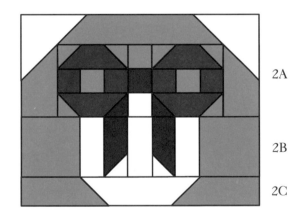

2A

2B

2C

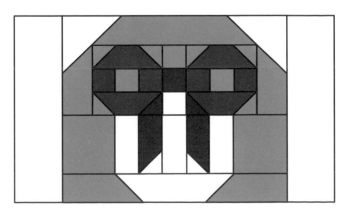

Sewing Row 3
"Bottom of
Wreath"

Use the Diagonal Sewing Technique. Trim and press seams toward background.

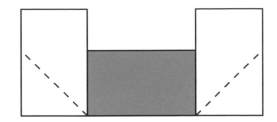

Sewing the Rows
Together

1. Use the Stabilizing Pin Technique to match the straight seams of Row 2 to the diagonal seams of Row 3.

2. Add Rows 1 and 4. Press seams as shown.

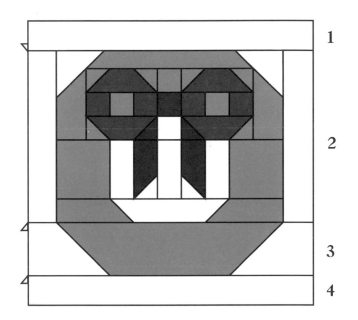

The Gift

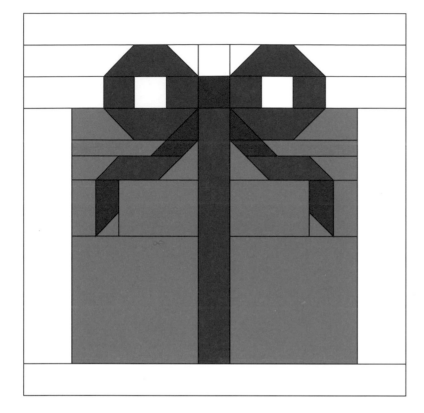

✂ Cutting Instructions

Cut from gift fabric:

(1) 2 ¼" x 45"--cut into:
(2) 2 ¼" x 3"	4r
(2) 1 ¾" x 1 ¾"	4m
(2) 1 ¼" x 2 ¼"	4k
(2) 1 ¼" x 1 ¼"	4q
(2) 1 ½" x 2 ¾"	4h
(2) 1" x 3 ¾"	4i
(2) 2 ¼" x 1 ½"	4o

(2) 4 ½" x 4 ½" 4t

Cut from medium bow fabric:

(1) 1 ½" x 45"--cut into:
(4) 1 ½" x 3 ½"	2c,4c
(4) 1 ½" x 1 ½"	3f
(2) 1 ¼" x 3 ¾"	4l
(1) 8 ½" x 1 ½"	4s

Cut from dark bow fabric:

(2) 2 ¼" x 1 ¼"	4p
(2) 1" x 2"	4j
(3) 1 ½" x 1 ½"	3g,4g

Cut from the background fabric:

(1) 2 ½" x 45"--cut into:
(2) 2 ½" x 13 ½"	1a,5a
(2) 8 ½" x 2 ½"	4n

(1) 1 ½" x 45"--cut into:
(2) 1 ½" x 4 ½"	2b
(2) 1 ½" x 3 ½"	3e
(5) 1 ½" x 1 ½"	2d,3d

O n the first Christmas, three wise kings traveled from afar to offer gifts to the Christ Child. They brought gold coins, the sweet spice frankincense, and aromatic myrrh. Peasants and shepherds also offered gifts of lambs, doves, a flute, and food for the parents of the new-born baby. Today we carry on this custom of gift giving at Christmas. Through giving, our gifts sustain the spirit of Christmas beyond the holiday. Our Christmas gifts are colorfully wrapped with grand bows and placed carefully under the tree to await the magic of Christmas morning. Like the Magi, we give our best to express our caring for another person, and our gifts symbolize the real Christmas gift for us all--the gift of a savior.

❏ Layout Diagram

Lay the cut pieces as shown in this diagram:

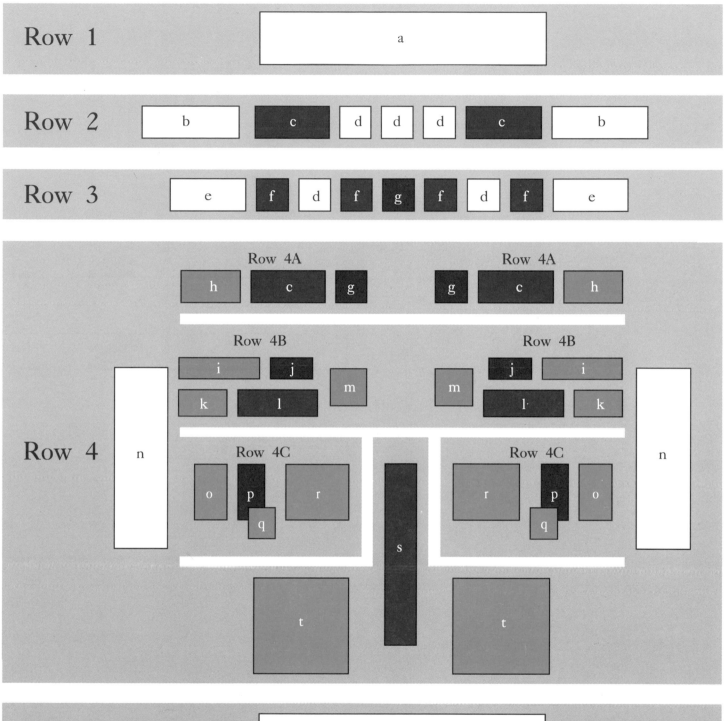

Sewing the Gift Block

Sewing Row 2

"Bow Top"

1. Use the Diagonal Sewing Technique. Trim and press seams toward background.

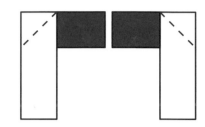

2. Use the Diagonal Sewing Technique to sew background squares (d) to the bow pieces. Trim and press seams toward background.

3. Add the remaining background square (d). Press seams toward center.

Sewing Row 3

"Bow Center"

Sew and press seams toward medium bow squares.

Sewing Row 4A

"Bow Bottom"

1. Use the Diagonal Sewing Technique to sew the gift pieces (h) to the medium bow pieces (c). Trim and press seams toward bow.

2. Use the Diagonal Sewing Technique to sew the dark bow squares (g) to the inside ends of medium bow pieces. Trim and press seams toward medium bow.

Sewing Row 4B

"Ties"

1. Use the Diagonal Sewing Technique to sew the gift pieces (i) to the dark bow pieces (j). Trim and press seams toward gift.

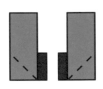

2. Use the Diagonal Sewing Technique to sew the gift pieces (k) to the medium bow pieces (l). Trim and press seams toward gift.

3. Sew the bow section from step 1 to the top of the bow section from step 2. Press seams down.

4. Use the Diagonal Sewing Technique to sew a gift square (m) to each bow section. Trim and press seams toward gift.

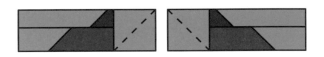

Sewing Row 4C

"Ends"

1. Use the Diagonal Sewing Technique to sew the gift squares (q) to the dark bow pieces (p). Trim and press seams toward bow.

2. Sew Row 4C. Press seams toward gift.

Sewing Row 4 Together

1. Use the Stabilizing Pin Technique sew Rows 4A, 4B, 4C. Press seams down.

   Center edges may need sliver trimming.

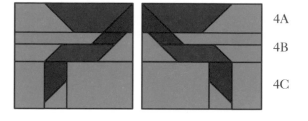

4A

4B

4C

2. Keep center edges even and sew the gift squares (t) to the bow sections. Press seams down.

   Outside edges need sliver trimming. The sections should measure 4 ½" wide.

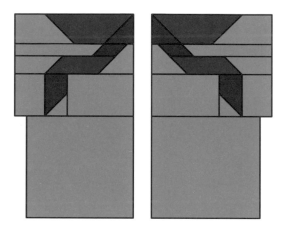

3. Matching the top edges and the horizontal seams, sew the long bow strip (s) between the bow sections. Press seam toward center.

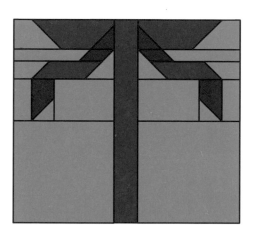

4. Add the background pieces. Press seams toward background.

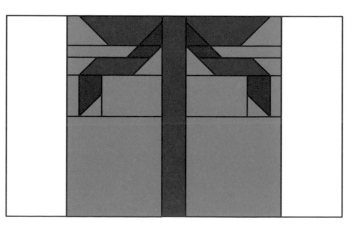

Sewing the Rows Together

1. Begin with Rows 2 and 3. Lock and pin the center straight seams. Use the Stabilizing Pin Technique to match the diagonal bow seams to the straight bow seams. Sew. Press seam away from center.

2. Match and pin the straight and diagonal seams of Row 3 to Row 4. Sew. Press seam toward gift.

3. Add Rows 1 and 5. Press seams as shown.

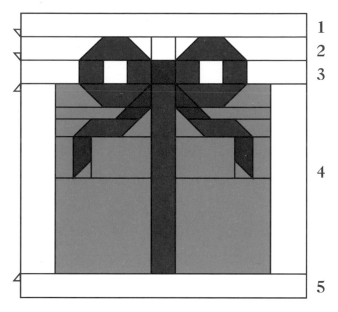

Squaring the Picture Blocks

The Picture Blocks are oversized at this point. Square each block to 12½" following these directions.

All blocks have distinct centers except:

The center of the Joy Block is half the distance from the outside edge of the "J" to the outside edge of the "Y".

The center of the Stocking Block is the middle of the cuff.

1. Place the 6¼" line of the 12½" Square Up ruler down the vertical center of the block.

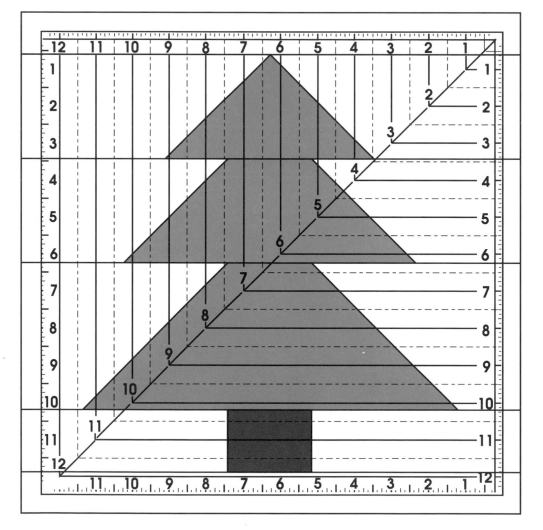

2. Keeping the ruler vertically centered, move it up and down until equal amounts of the first and last row, approximately 1¼" to 1⅜", remain at the top and bottom of the block.

3. Trim the right side and the top edge.

4. Give the block a half turn, replace the ruler and trim the remaining two sides.

The Chain Blocks

Cutting the Chain Blocks

Cut from background fabric:

(10) 2½" x 45" background strips

(10) 4½" x 45" background strips

(4) 8½" x 45" background strips

Cut from chain fabric:

(3) 4½" x 45" chain strips

(10) 2½" x 45" chain strips

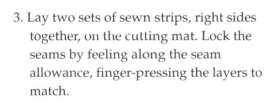 Sewing the 72 Four-Patch Squares

Use:

(10) 2½" x 45" background strips
(10) 2½" x 45" chain strips

Use the scant ¼" seam allowance.

1. Line up the long edges, right sides together, and assembly-line sew the background strips to the chain strips.

2. Press seams towards the chain strip.

   Make certain there are no folds at the seam line.

3. Lay two sets of sewn strips, right sides together, on the cutting mat. Lock the seams by feeling along the seam allowance, finger-pressing the layers to match.

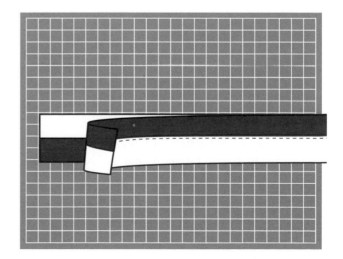

4. Right angle cut the left edge to straighten and remove the selvages.

5. Layer cut a pair every 2½", for a total of (72) 2½" layered pieces.

   As you cut, place the 2½" paired pieces onto the flannel board to transfer them to the sewing machine.

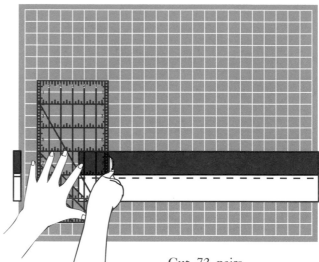

Cut 72 pairs

6. Pick up the first pair keeping the chain fabric at the top. Lock the center seams.

7. Assembly-line sew all 2½" pairs.

8. Clip the connecting threads. Press seams.

9. Set aside 4 Four-Patch Squares for the Corner Blocks to be sewn later.

Sewing the 34 Four-Patch Strips

Use:

(68) Four-Patch Squares
(4) 4½" x 45" background strips

1. Divide the (68) Four-Patch Squares into two equal stacks of 34 each.

2. Assembly-line sew one stack of Four-Patch Squares, right sides together and seams down, to the background strips.

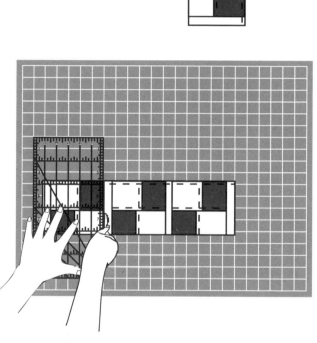

3. Cut apart between the Four-Patch Squares, making two cuts if they are not closely butted.

4. Assembly-line sew the remaining half of the Four-Patch Squares, right sides together, to the opposite side of the Background Squares.

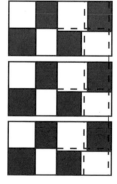

5. Press seams toward the Four-Patch Squares.

Sewing the 21 Center Strips

Use:

(5) 4½" x 45" background strips
(3) 4½" x 45" chain strips

1. Cut one background strip and one chain strip in half.

   Set aside one half chain strip for the Corner Blocks to be sewn later.

2. Arrange the background strips and chain strips in stacks of 2½ strips each.

3. Assembly-line sew the background strips, right sides together, to the chain strips.

4. Open the strips. Assembly-line sew the remaining stack of background strips, right sides together, to the chain strips.

5. Clip the connecting threads. Press seams toward chain.

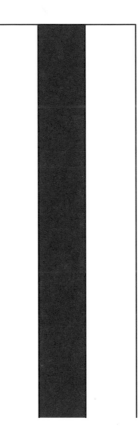

6. Lay a strip on the cutting mat and right angle cut the left edge to straighten and remove the selvages.

7. Cut every 4½".

   (21) 4½" Center Strips are needed.

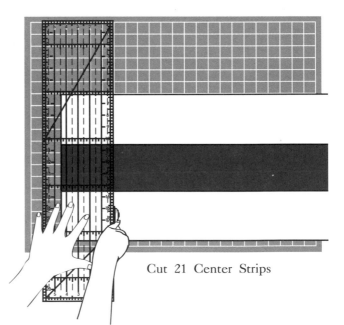

Cut 21 Center Strips

Sewing the 13 Chain Blocks

Use:

(26) Four-Patch Strips
(13) Center Strips

1. Divide the Four-Patch Strips into two equal stacks and arrange with Center Strips.

2. Assembly-line sew the Center Strips, right sides together, to one stack of Four-Patch Strips.

   Sew with the Center Strip on top. Match top and bottom edges, and lock the seams as you sew.

3. Assembly-line sew the remaining stack of Four-Patch Strips, right sides together, to the opposite side of the Center Strips.

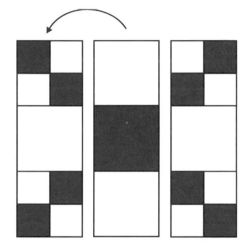

4. Clip the connecting threads. Press seams toward Center Strip.

5. Chain Blocks should measure approximately 12 ½" square.

   If Chain Blocks are less than 12¼", trim the Picture Blocks to that Chain Block measurement.

Sewing the 8 Border Chain Blocks

Use:

(8) Four-Patch Strips
(8) Center Strips

1. Assembly-line sew the Center Strips, right sides together, to the Four-Patch Strips.

2. Clip the connecting threads. Press seams toward Center Strips.

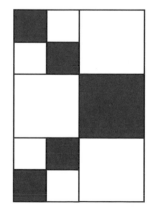

Sewing the 4 Corner Chain Blocks

Use:

(1) 4½" x 45" background strip, cut in half
(½) 4½" x 45" chain strip, set aside earlier
(4) Four-Patch Squares, set aside earlier

1. Sew a half strip of background, right sides together, to the half strip of chain.

2. Press seam toward the chain strip.

3. Right angle cut the left edge to straighten and remove selvages.

4. Cut four 4½" pieces. Set aside.

Cut 4 Center Pieces

5. Sew the four Four-Patch Squares, right sides together, to the remaining half strip of background.

6. Using a 6" x 6" ruler, cut apart between the Four-Patch Squares.

7. Press seams toward Four-Patch Squares.

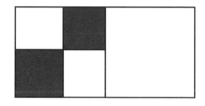

Cut 4 Four-Patch Pieces

8. Assembly-line sew the Center Pieces, right sides together, to the Four-Patch Pieces.

9. Press seams toward Center Pieces.

Cutting the Border Rectangles

Remove selvages and cut the (4) 8½" x 45" background strips into (12) 8½" x 12½" pieces.

Sewing the Quilt Top Together

Laying Out the Quilt

1. Lay out the 12 Picture Blocks, 13 Chain Blocks, 8 Border Chain Blocks, 4 Corner Chain Blocks, and 12 Border Rectangles according to the illustration.

There is no set layout for the 12 Picture Blocks. At this point you will want to play with the 12 Picture Blocks and rearrange them until you are satisfied with their placement.

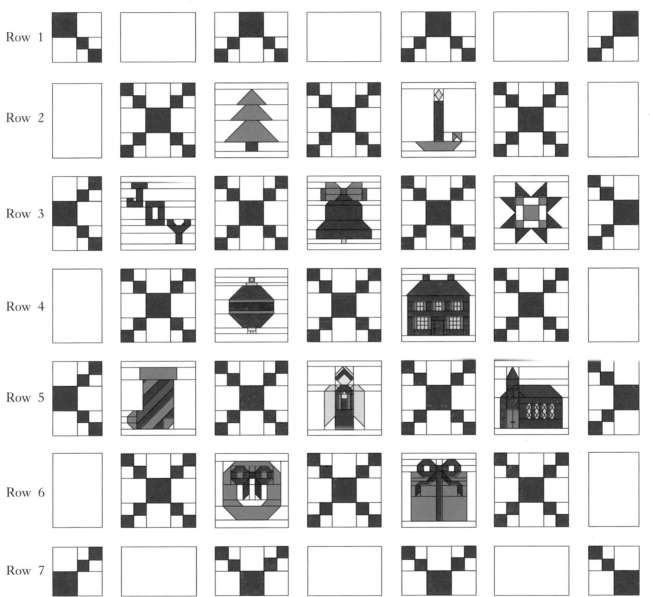

Sewing the Horizontal Rows

Pin the blocks, matching the outer edges, as you sew each horizontal row. Stretch or ease blocks to fit. Press seams toward Chain Blocks.

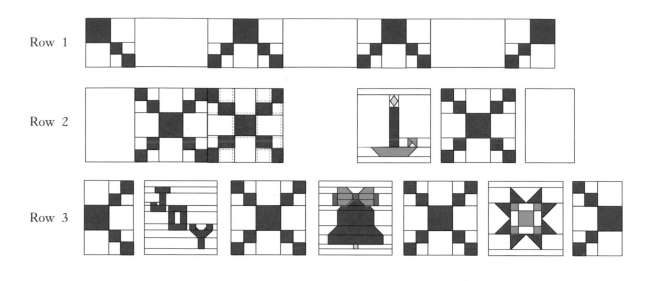

Sewing the Horizontal Rows Together

Lay out the horizontal rows of the quilt top, and make sure the sewn rows are arranged properly.

Flip Row 1 down onto Row 2, right sides together. Pin vertical seams at each intersection. Seams should lock and go in opposite directions. Sew Rows 1 and 2 together, stretching or easing blocks to fit.

Sew the remaining rows together in pairs--Row 3 onto 4, Row 5 onto 6. *Row 7 can be sewn to the last pair.* Press seams flat, and then press seams down. Sew the pairs of rows together and press the quilt top.

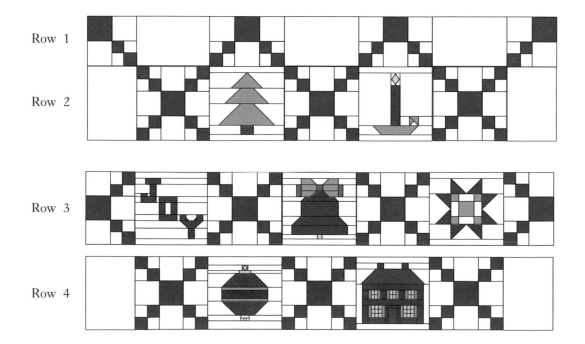

Marking Holly Designs

If you wish to free motion quilt, trace the holly design onto the quilt either before or after layering with batting and backing. Refer to page 82 for more information on Free Motion Quilting

1. Lay the template plastic over the holly design and trace the design. Flip the plastic and trace the design again for the other half.

2. So the template remains in one piece, cut along the outside edges of the berries and the holly. Draw the inside of the berries on the template.

3. Center the template on the "triangular" areas along the outside edge of the quilt and lightly trace around the template. Draw the berries freehand.

Center Line

79

Finishing the Quilt

Preparing the Backing

1. If piecing, fold the 5 yards of backing crosswise and cut into two equal pieces. If you made a custom size quilt, you may need to adjust these measurements.

2. Tear off the selvages and seam the backing pieces together. Press seam in one direction.

3. Embroider your name, city, state, and date on the backing with hand stitching or machine writing.

Piecing the Bonded Batting

1. If the batting needs to be pieced to get the desired size, cut and butt the two straight edges closely without overlapping.

2. Whipstitch the edges together with a double strand of thread. Do not pull the threads tightly as this will create a hard ridge visible on the outside of the quilt.

Adding the Backing

1. Stretch out the backing right side down on a large floor area or table. Tape down on the floor area or clamp onto a table with large binder clips.

2. Place and smooth out the batting on top. Lay the quilt top right side up and centered on top of the batting. Completely smooth and stretch all layers until they are flat. Tape or clamp securely. The backing and batting should extend at least 2" on all sides.

3. Place safety pins along both sides of the chain, around the picture blocks, and around the holly design. Begin pinning in the center and work to the outside.

4. Trim the backing and batting to within 2" of the outside edge of the quilt.

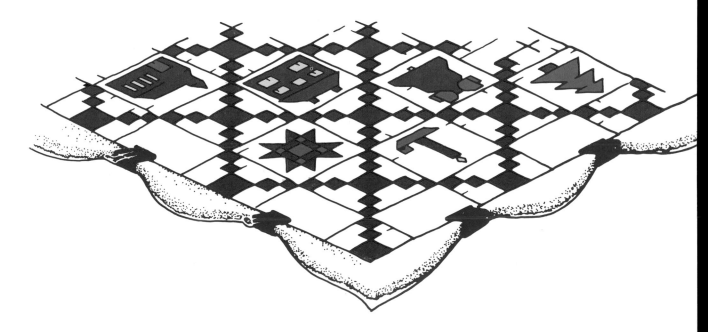

Machine Quilting

The machine quilting will be done in three stages on this quilt.

I. Machine Quilting the Diagonal Chain

Stitching along the diagonal lines of the chain with a walking foot is the easiest machine quilting.

Mark the diagonal lines with a hard sliver of soap or 1/4" masking tape. Position the masking tape just to the left of the intended diagonal stitching lines.

Use a soft nylon invisible thread or thread to match the chain fabric in the top of your machine and regular thread in the bobbin to match the backing. Loosen the top tension, and lengthen your stitch to 8-10 stitches per inch, or a #4.

It is a good idea to straight pin the length of each diagonal quilting line before stitching.

1. Tightly roll the quilt on the diagonal from the outside in toward the middle. Hold this roll with bicycle clips or pins.

2. Slide this roll into the keyhole of the sewing machine.

3. Unroll, roll, and machine quilt on all diagonal lines.

II. Outline Quilting the Picture Blocks

Outline quilt ¼" away from the outside edges of the Picture Blocks. Use the edge of the walking foot as a guide. Use invisible thread or regular thread to match the background fabric in the top and thread to match the backing in the bobbin.

For easier handling, start at the top center of each picture and outline one side to the bottom center. Then return to the top center and outline the opposite side.

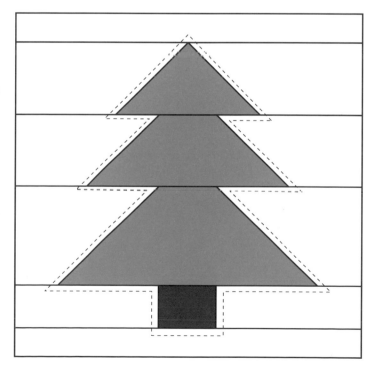

III. Free Motion Quilting the Holly Designs

This is a more advanced method of machine quilting using a darning foot. You have the freedom to stitch forward, backwards, and to the sides without the use of a presser foot or feed dogs. However, this method requires practice.

Refer to your instruction manual for directions on how to darn with your machine. You will need to use a darning foot, and drop or cover the feed dogs with a plate. Practice before attempting the free motion quilting.

No stitch length is required as you control the length of the stitch. Lower the speed of your machine if possible. Use a fine needle and a little hole throat plate. Use invisible thread or regular thread in the top and thread to match your backing in the bobbin.

1. Roll the quilt to one Border Rectangle and hold in place with bicycle clips.

   Before you begin to sew, study the diagram showing the direction to free motion quilt.

2. Bring the bobbin thread up at the starting point. Lower the needle into the quilt and drop the foot. The quilt should move freely under the darning foot. Move the fabric very slowly and take a few tiny stitches to lock them. Snip off the tails of the threads.

3. With your eyes watching the line ahead of the needle, and your fingertips stretching the fabric and acting as a quilting hoop, move the fabric in a steady motion while the machine is running at a constant speed. Do not move the fabric fast as this will break the needle. Keep the top of the block in the same position by moving the fabric underneath the needle side to side, and forward and backward.

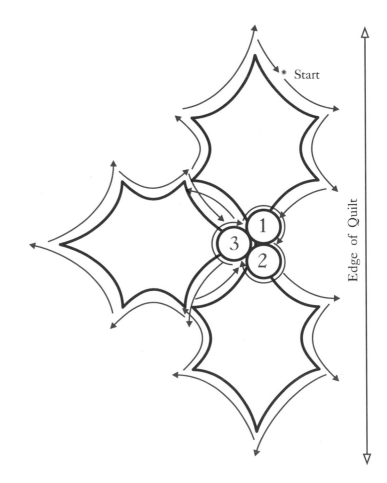

4. As shown, start with the right hand leaf now in the upper position. Sew down the right edge, clockwise around berries 1 and 2, complete the lower leaf, berry 3, the center leaf and the remainder of the first leaf. **As you sew the berries clockwise, you will be sewing over stitches in order to sew the entire motif without stopping.**

5. Lock off with tiny stitches and clip the threads.

Binding the Quilt

I. Preparing the Binding

1. Cut eight binding strips 5½" x 45".

2. Remove selvages. Join strips in pairs. Trim and press seams to one side.

2. Fold in half lengthwise, wrong sides together. Press.

II. Stitching the Binding to the Quilt

Use:

A Walking Foot or Even Feed Attachment
10 Stitches to the Inch
Thread to Match the Binding

1. In each corner of the quilt, mark a dot ¼" from each edge.

2. Place a pin 2" from one end of the binding strip. Match the pin to the ¼" dot, laying the raw edge of the binding along the raw edge of the quilt top. Stitch through all layers, anchoring by backstitching or stitching in place. Stitch to the dot at the other end, backstitch, then remove from the machine. Leave 2" free, then cut the strip off.

3. Turn the quilt to the next side. Leaving two 2" ends hanging loose at each corner, repeat sewing the binding to each side. Make sure that you begin to sew at the dot in the corner, pushing the previously sewn strip out of the way.

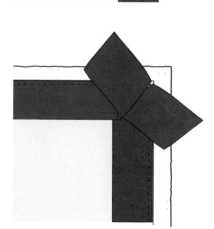

III. Mitering the Corners

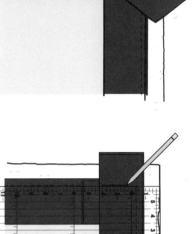

1. At one corner, fold the 2" excess of one strip back on itself. Lay the other strip on top. Lay a ruler along the horizontal stitching line and mark a pencil line across the top strip starting at the fold and ending at the vertical stitching line.

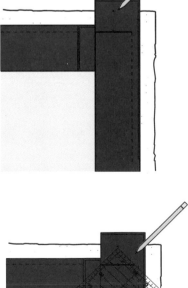

2. Measure the distance of the pencil mark, from the folded edge of the strip to the stitching line. Place a dot mid-way on this line. It should be about 1¼" from each end.

3. Measure up from the dot, toward the cut end of the strip, 1¼" and place another dot. Draw a line from the folded edge to the last dot you made and from that dot to the stitching line. It will look like a triangle.

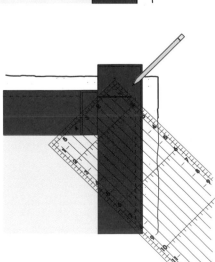

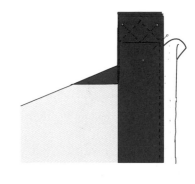

4. Bring together the excess of the strips, making the folded edges even. Pin along the drawn triangle, being careful not to catch the quilt with the pin at the seam.

5. Stitch a "V" along the triangle from the folded edge to the top point, pivot, and continue along the triangle to the stitching line. Be sure to backstitch at each end.

6. Repeat with the other three corners.

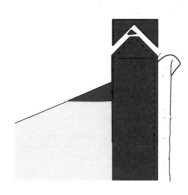

7. Trim the triangle, ¼" from the stitching line and across the point.

8. Place ruler's 1" line along the stitching and trim the batting and backing to 1" from the stitching line. Do not cut off the binding triangles.

Casing to hang quilt (Optional): Measure the width of the trimmed quilt and subtract 4". Cut a 6" wide strip at that measurement. Make a ½" hem on the short sides. Fold the strip lengthwise to form a 3" folded casing. Center the casing on the top back side of the quilt with the raw edges even with the trimmed quilt. Pin and stitch within the seam allowance. Hand stitch the fold to the backing.

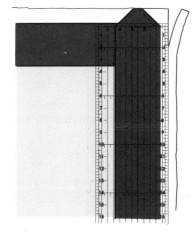

9. Turn the mitered corners right sides out, fold over to the back of the quilt and pin the binding to the back.

IV. Finishing the Binding

Choose one method for finishing the binding.

1. Hand stitch the binding to the back of the quilt.

2. Machine stitch in the depth of the seam from the front side of the quilt catching the binding on the back.

Creative One Block Projects

21" Square   Patricia Knoechel

Oh! Christmas Tree!

Trimmed with purchased packages, ribbon roses and bows, this embellished tree block would grace any holiday home or office. Garlands of pearls, a large floral border, and a treeskirt cut from decorator fabric add a Victorian flavor. The loose, scalloped treeskirt edge is trimmed with lace, and the straight edge is sewn into the seam allowance. The narrow border is cut at 1½" and the wider at 3½". Braid glued to the wallhanging adds a holiday sparkle.

Candle in the Window

To warm the heart, this candle block is lit with a gold lame' flame. The background is a midnight blue seen through lacy curtains attached in the seam of the border. Ribbon, gold cording and a sprig of holly complete the setting. The burgundy candle holder fabric is repeated in the first border cut at 1¾" and the binding. A stripe fabric border, cut at 5", is mitered.

25" Square   Patricia Knoechel

21" Square   Patricia Knoechel

Joy Banner

A Joy Block is transformed into a tasseled wallhanging heralding the holiday season. Star-studded borders are cut at 2". The patchwork border is made of 5 fabrics 2½" by 22", sewn together, topstitched with trim at the seam, and cut into 2½" segments. The hanging loops are cut at 5" x 4", folded lengthwise and sewn. Bottom tassels are 4½" strips cut at 9", 11", and 14", folded in half, and sewn in a point. Pin the loops and tassels to the border and finish with a "quick turn." Add gold trim or bells for a royal touch.

Sounds of Christmas

The red, green and white tones of the Bell Block reverberate in traditional holiday colors. The 9-patch border is cut from 1½" strips. A 3" border and binding frame the quilt. Hang this wall quilt with an optional bow made from a 6" x 45" strip, folded in half lengthwise, sewn and tied. The ends are sewn to the top edge.

23" Square   Eleanor Burns

25" Square   Eleanor Burns

The Star of Bethlehem

"Fussy cutting" a poinsettia center and setting the block on point adds sophistication to the simple but elegant Star Block. The completed block is squared to 13". Two 10" squares cut in half on the diagonals frame the block. The 2¼" border strips and four-patch corners of 2¼" pieced triangles capture this brilliant star.

Victorian Ornament

Framed in a 3" polished cotton floral and decorated with old fashioned braid, tapestry ribbon and lace, this Ornament Block takes on the elegance of times long ago. Topstitch the embellishments to the decorative center piece before adding the background. Repeat the ornament fabric in the 1" narrow border.

19" x 24"   Eleanor Burns

19" x 24"   Eleanor Burns

Festive Christmas Stocking

This cheery Stocking is "stuffed" with holiday decorations, hot glued at the opened top edge of the cuff.

Substitute a 5" by 13½" strip for Row 1. When sewing Rows 1 and 2 together, machine baste the cuff. Press that seam open and flat. Edgestitch the cuff. After the 1½" and 3" borders are added and the quilt is finished, remove the basting to form a pocket for the ornaments.

22" x 25"   Joann Osborn

Home for Country Christmas

The perfect tile fabric for the roof and checked fabric for the chimney and shutters add charm and warmth to the Home Block. Paned windows are aglow with wreaths, tree and children cut from fabric and fused.

The patchwork pinetrees take you into the woods and home for Christmas. Cut a 2¾" x 3½" rectangle into a triangle with 2¾" height and 3½" base. Sew 2" light background strips to each side. Trim the tree to 2½" x 3". Sew one 1½" trunk strip and two 1¼" background strips together, and then cut them into 1⅛" segments to complete the tree. Finish with 2" and 3" borders.

Church in Winter Wonderland

The perfect 14" x 18" scenic fabric completes the serenity of this snowy scene. Eliminate the background, and substitute white flannel for the roof and steeple. Cut the steeple into a triangle. Cut ¼" from the Diagonal Sewing line on the roof (i) and church (f) for seam allowance. After construction, place the church right sides to the fusible side of non-woven, iron-on interfacing. Stitch around the church, leaving the bottom open. Trim, turn right side out and position on the bottom edge of the scenic fabric. Press and blind hem stitch with invisible thread. Edgestitch a 4" x 18" piece of batting for snow. A 1½" dark border and a 3" light border add to the brightness. Glowing white pearls in the trees light up the night surrounding the church.

24" Square   Patricia Knoechel

A Trio of Angels

These angelic visitors herald the message of Christmas. Feathery wings and gown touched with gold add grace to these spiritual symbols. Each block is squared to 9½" x 12". Rainbow border squares are 1½" strips, sewn together lengthwise and cut into 1½" segments. An outer white border cut at 1" crowns the wallhanging.

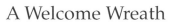

30" x 16"   Andrea Hong

A Welcome Wreath

A holly fabric embellished with scarlet bead berries and tied in a bright red bow becomes a holiday wreath to welcome visitors at your doorstep. Machine quilting using a stippling technique gives added dimension to the wreath. It is finished with borders of 1½" and 3".

20" Square   Eleanor Burns

All Wrapped Up for Christmas!

This gift is wrapped in Christmas red and tied in a green bow. A tiny border and the hanging loops are made from ¾" strips. Nine-Patch corners compliment the 1¾" borders and seminole piecing, made from 1½" strips.

21" Square   Carole Wells